MW01257581

OPAL

Identification

and

Value

by

Paul B. Downing, Ph.D.

Majestic Press, Inc.
Estes Park, CO

DEDICATED TO: *Rudy Weber* and *Len Cram,* without whose help this book could not have been completed, and to *Richard & Mary Lou Osmond,* who opened doors in Australia I might never have knocked on.

Cover photographs by Rudy G. Weber.
Graphics by Finlay Graphics

First Printing 1992, Second Printing 1995.
Printed in the United States of America

Majestic Press, Inc.
P. O. Box 2265
Estes Park, CO 80517-2265
(800) 468-0324

ISBN 0-9625311-2-X

Table of Contents

Author's Note

My goal as I set out to do this book more than three years ago, was to produce a methodology for valuing opals which worked. But more important it had to work the same way for every person who used it. Thus, it was necessary to combine definitions of the various characteristics of an opal with a visual, measurable and reproducible criteria. It needed to be visual so that each person who used the definition gained the same sense of meaning from the words. A picture is worth a thousand words, especially when describing opal characteristics. Measurable criteria had to be developed so that each stone could be objectively characterized. The criteria had to be reproducible so that each individual using the valuing methodology employed the same meaning for each item.

Photographs were the only way. I am fortunate to know two excellent opal photographers, *Len Cram* and *Rudy Weber*, who have large libraries of pictures of opals of all types and characteristics. Each has access to some of the best opals found in Australia. Their photo libraries are an attempt to chronicle this exciting stone. Just to see them is a real treat. They are wonderful.

I searched through their libraries and selected pictures that would best illustrate the characteristics I needed for visual criteria. I did not always select the most beautiful picture, although there is plenty of beauty within these pages. Rather, I selected pictures for the utilitarian purpose of adding a visual to the definitions to be contained in this book. Without the help of Rudy and Len this book could not have been done. I am deeply in their debt.

Originally I was going to make my own estimates of value and set up a panel of experts to produce periodic updates. The more I though about that, the more work it seemed. Then my wonderful wife, Bobbi, suggested a simple solution. Why not use someone else's estimates of market value? The someone else was Richard Drucker and his market assessment of colored stones called *The Guide*. Terrific idea. Richard and his panel were already doing estimates of opal value and updating them periodically. Exactly what I needed, leaving me time to research more thoroughly the individual characteristics. Richard and I talked and he agreed to let me use his data. Again, I couldn't do it without him.

The result of using *The Guide* as the basis for value is that this book never becomes outdated. To get a current reading of market value all you have to do is consult the current issue of *The Guide*. Then you can use the prices it contains with the methodology presented in this book to obtain the latest market estimate of the value of any opal.

The whole book is set up with one goal in mind. I want any user, anywhere in the world, to identify all the relevant characteristics of a particular opal in exactly the same way. The book is, unfortunately, quite detailed. This detail is needed so that each reader understands the subtle differences that can have a significant affect on value.

To make this detail a little less difficult to follow, I have broken down the process. The book instructs step-by-step, one characteristic at a time. When all the characteristics have been explained, I show how they are put together to form an estimate of value.

I have attempted to make the book complete by covering all sources of opal that appear on the market from Australia, Mexico, America, Brazil, Honduras and Hungary. I have covered all types too, including solid opal (black, white, and crystal), boulder opal, matrix opal, carved opal, doublets, triplets, synthetics and simulated. However, new sources appear yearly. Fortunately, the characteristics that make opal valuable, even opal from new sources, are covered in this book. Using these characteristics you should be able to estimate the market reaction to that new opal from Timbuktu.

It is important to realize that the use of the terms I define here have evolved in the industry over time and by word of mouth. It is inevitable that others will use or visualize these terms a little differently. Hopefully this book will be a first step toward a common and consistent terminology. Remember that definitions are never wrong—they are just different. I hope to narrow these differences.

I realize that the opal market is alive and well, and thus always in a state of change. I cannot hope to anticipate the future.

Rather, I have done my best to give the most accurate picture of the market at this time.

To do this I have consulted with various opal experts. I have had the privilege of sitting and kibitzing with the Opal Advisory Service of the Lightning Ridge Miners Association on numerous occasions. I have discussed pricing and this project at length with various opal experts in Australia, including Richard Osmond, Joy Clayton, Greg Sherman and John Traurig of Sydney; Ted Priester and Len Cram of Lightning Ridge; Ewe Barfuss of Yowah; Andrew Cody of Melbourne; Andrew Shelley of Coober Pedy; Stafford Scott of Mintabie; Mario Anic of Andamooka; and many others. Several opal cutters in Hong Kong have been most helpful, especially Sunny Li and Peter Su.

In the United States I have consulted with David Baitel, Martin Bell, Tony Dabdoub, Richard Drucker, Brian Franks, Keith Griffin, Glen and Keith Hodson, Bill Maison, Gerry Manning, and Charlie Smith, among others.

None of these very helpful people agree with me completely, but I have taken their advice to the best of my ability.

Presentations of these ideas at various meetings of the Accredited Gemologists Association and at the GIA International Symposium have helped me clarify and refine this book. My early article, "Evaluating Cut Opal", appeared in the December, 1987 issue of *Rock & Gem*. This article was stimulated by a prior attempt at a pricing system put out by the American Opal Society.

Specific detailed reviews of drafts of parts or all of this book were done by Len Cram, Richard Drucker, Pat Dunnigan, Richard Osmond and Ted Priester.

Without the help of all these people I could not have created this book. Still, I must accept all the blame for the remaining errors.

I hope you find this book helpful, and maybe a little entertaining from time to time.

Thanks,

Paul B. Downing
Tallahassee, FL
January, 1992

Len Cram

Magnificent Gems Like This Black Opal
Are The Pride of Australia.

Chapter 1

Characteristics and Value

It is widely recognized in the opal industry both in Australia and the United States that the use of terminology among opal dealers and jewelers is imprecise and confused. In my travels and lectures I have been approached on numerous occasions to clarify the meaning of a term or to explain why one opal is more highly valued than another. Others in the industry, both in Australia and the United States, tell me they face the same questions. As one prominent Australian opal dealer puts it, "Experts will differ in some aspects of classification and nomenclature. Unfortunately, at this stage there is no industry standard, although this is on the agenda of the proposed (Australian) Gemstone Industry Council.[1]" Trained jewelers and gemologists explain that they feel a significant gap in their knowledge of opals. What is needed, they say, is a single source which defines terms so that all members of the industry will use them consistently. This book is my effort at doing so.

The goal of this book can be stated simply:

GOAL:

To present a methodology for identifying and valuing opals that produces accurate and identical evaluations when used by various individuals at any time or location.

---

[1]A. Cody, *Australian Precious Opals*, Andrew Cody Pty. Ltd., 1991, p. 7.

This is a rather ambitious goal, I know, but goals are supposed to be a little out of reach. To achieve my goal the following steps are necessary:

Step One: Develop visual, measurable and reproducible criteria for the various characteristics that determine an opal's value using photographs and other visual aids.

Step Two: Derive a common and consistent terminology for opal characteristics in consultation with opal experts worldwide.

Step Three: Present a step-by-step process of identifying each characteristic which influences the value of an opal.

Step Four: Relate these characteristics to value in a consistent manner using the *Opal Evaluation Form*.

Step Five: Tie these characteristics to a current assessment of market value: *The Guide*.

Step Six: Cover all types of opals including solids, boulder opal, man-enhanced opals, man-made opals and simulants. Cover all major sources to show how each source fits into the methodology.

The organization of this book follows these six steps. It is an interesting and educational journey. Remember to stop and admire the opal along the way.

Characteristics and Value

"Wow, what a gorgeous stone!" That was my first reaction as the miner proudly presented his opal. Brilliant flashes of red, orange, green and blue leapt to my eye. These colors were set off on a dense, dark background. As I moved the stone, I noted that the colors flashed in a square harlequin pattern. The brightness of the fire held up as I moved the stone away from the light. In fact, it got a little brighter. While the stone was a little flat, that was not a serious problem as the opal was a real beauty. No doubt about it, I was holding a rare and unique gem opal. I wanted it!

Now my problem began. Was this outstanding stone worth the major price the miner was asking? Could I pay that price and sell the stone in the United States? Almost automatically my mental computer started its calculations. Solid black opal with brilliant fire. Red multicolor fire in a rare harlequin pattern. Well cut but flat with no visible imperfections. Large but not too big for jewelry. Clackity-clack my brain went and the answer tumbled into my conscious mind. I should be able to buy this stone for about X dollars per carat.

How did I come up with that number? Experience told me that the particular combination of characteristics found in this stone corresponded with similar characteristics in other opals which sold for about X dollars per carat. While no two opals are identical, each has various characteristics in common with other stones. I have developed a sense for how these characteristics combine to create value. The experience of seeing lots of opals and their associated prices has programmed weightings for these characteristics into my mind. In this book, my goal is to search through that internal program and teach you about the factors I use to determine market value.

> ## Opal is a difficult stone to value.

Determining the market value of an opal is a complex task. In fact, opal is considered the most difficult of all stones to value. First, there are no two stones alike. Each has a unique combination of characteristics which set it apart from all other opals. Second, preferences for stones with various characteristics will differ from one person to another. Thus, one person may rate a stone as more valuable because it contains characteristics they like, while another may dislike that type of opal and, thus, value it less highly. In my

Photograph 1-1   *Rudy G. Weber*

No two opals are alike.
It pays to know the differences.

experience even experts who make their living buying and selling opals can differ by 15% in their estimate of an opal's price. This 15% variation is true for more standard opals called *commercial* stones—the types of stones seen in mass produced jewelry. On rare occasions where a stone is particularly unique or unusual the variation can become as large as 50%. Third, a very few people in the world have occasion to see more than a few opals each year, especially the higher quality stones.

When a person is not in continual day-to-day contact with a variety of opals, they may lose track of the importance of various characteristics. This does not mean they are incompetent. It is just not possible to keep all the factors which affect opal value in one's mind when the information is used on an occasional basis. Even opal experts who are in daily contact with a wide variety of opal often use special self-developed guides to help them in valuing opals. In fact, it was the observation of others using visual criteria that got me started thinking about publishing such a criteria set. The problem was that each dealer had his or her own way of doing things and each was somewhat at odds with that of other dealers.

People use terminology in different ways. One may call a stone a black while another may call it a semi-black. Other terms are also used inconsistently among dealers.   One of the tasks I have set

> ## Terminology is used in different ways.

for myself in this book is to produce a set of terms which all persons can use consistently. To do this it was necessary to develop definitions for these terms. But this was not enough. I also needed to develop visual and reproducible criteria to fit with those definitions. For only in this way can we be sure that everybody is using a term to mean the same thing. Finally, I have developed a simple methodology for relating those characteristics of an opal defined by these visual criteria to market value.

It is also important to note that I could not hope to succeed in this effort without careful consultation with others. Consequently I have discussed the definitions and weightings I have dredged out of my mind with opal experts in all the opal fields and major marketing centers in Australia, Hong Kong and the United States. While I have been the final arbitrator, in a very real sense this has been a joint effort of many people, each heavily involved in the opal market.

Basic Step-By-Step Methodology

What I am offering here is a methodology which will allow you to identify an opal accurately as to all the characteristics that determine market value. This methodology will take you step-by-step so there is little chance you will make a mistake. Accompanying each step along the way you will have visual guides as well as descriptions to show you what to look for. It is these visual guides that make this methodology successful.

> ## Please do not skip a step.

It is easy to forget to look for something that can have a significant effect on value, so please do not skip a step.

After you have completely identified the relevant characteristics of an opal, value can be determined from several alternative value guides. The main source of value I employ here is *The Guide.*[2] I believe it to be the most accurate and up-to-date reference on opal value now available in the United States. But I do not suggest it is the only source available. Nor do I always agree with it. Use whatever source you are comfortable with. Keep this in mind though. Any value reference is only successful if you have accurately identified the characteristics of the opal in question. It is important that you go through the steps I suggest carefully and completely.

It is important to use a source such as *The Guide* that is updated periodically because opal prices continue to rise.[3] Opal prices have risen at least 20% per year over the past ten years and are expected to continue to go up.

While I have developed objective criteria for determining the characteristics of each opal, it is inevitable that judgment will come into play. You will be asked to judge the effect of inclusions, patterns, directionality, shape, etc. on the beauty of the opal. I will give you as much help here as I can. But while such judgments can be informed by what I say here, they are complex in a world where no two opals are ever exactly alike. It takes the experience of dealing with thousands of opals to fully develop this judgment. Even then, as I have pointed out, opinions will differ.

Experienced and successful opal dealers have developed this judgment to a fine art. Frequently an opal expert will look at a stone and tell you it is something special. But if you ask them why, they may not be able to explain it in detail. They have internalized this judgment over years of seeing stones of all varieties. It is not uncommon for such an expert to be able to identify not only the location where the opal was found, but the year a stone was mined. He may recall that this type of pattern or background was found only at one location. The distinguishing differences are often subtle.

This book cannot replace those years of experience. Fortunately, you do not need to know all the details gathered over

---

[2]*The Guide* is available from the publisher Gemworld International, Inc., 630 Dundee Road, Suite 235, Northbrook, IL 60062, (708) 564-0555.

[3]Australian Gem Industry Association, "Opal Prices: Still Going Up," *Jewelers' Circular - Keystone*, August, 1991, pp. 148-152.

those years. The basic characteristics determine over 98% of the value of a typical opal. After having read and thoroughly digested this book and its methodology, you will be far better informed about these characteristics and their effect on value than the vast majority of gemologists. You can become an opal expert with consistent and continuous exposure to a wide variety of stones. I believe that this book will help you get there faster. This is because it will give you a solid framework on which to build your judgment through experience. Even if you don't become an opal expert, this methodology will keep you up to date and allow you to produce consistent and accurate valuations.

Opal Terminology

Terminology in the opal industry is complex. Understanding this terminology is even more complex because there is not complete agreement among miners and dealers as to the meaning of a term. Sometimes the differences are subtle, but in two areas they may be substantial. Just how dark the base of a stone must be to call it a black opal is one of the areas where differences in definition may be substantial. I employ a visual standard here which is a reproduction of one produced by the Lightning Ridge Miners Association's Opal Advisory Service.

Another area of difference is the definition of patterns, particularly the rare pattern called "Harlequin." Some use a very narrow definition while others place a very broad interpretation on the term. In the definitions provided for all characteristics affecting opal value, I have attempted to capture the general meaning in the trade. To develop this general meaning I have discussed terminology with many opal experts in Australia, the United States and Hong Kong. In addition, I have gathered information from the GIA (Gemological Institute of America) and its Australian equivalent the AGIA (Australian Gem Industry Association), as well as the Lightning Ridge Miners Association. Where there are significant differences among experts on the meaning of a term, I will point out these differences and explain.

Objective Criteria

In order for this methodology to work it is necessary to employ objective criteria. For various valuers to characterize a particular opal in the same fashion, they must use the same criteria. Thus, the criteria must be reproducible. The beauty of an opal is its visual impact. No combination of words can fully describe this look. I know; I tried. Words are just not sufficient. To make sure all valuers are using the same terms to describe the same characteristics a visual criteria is necessary. What is needed is a set of photographs.

I am very fortunate to know two men who are spectacular opal photographers. It is exceedingly difficult to photograph opals so the characteristics that are important to value are evident. These two men have mastered the art after a considerable time learning its ins and outs. Len Cram is a miner, artist, and author who has spent all his time since World War II in the opal fields of Queensland and Lightning Ridge. Rudy Weber is a second-generation Lightning Ridge opal miner who now photographs full-time in Sydney. Between them there are very few opals of significance produced in the last twenty years that have not been carefully photographed and preserved. I have been privileged to search through their vast libraries of slides to select the very best photographs to illustrate all the characteristics which give opal value. My methodology would not work without their expert photography.

There is one very important characteristic which photographs cannot fully identify. That is the brightness of the fire coming back from the stone. While I have attempted to portray brightness in the photographs I present in Chapter 6, this is less than successful. To solve this problem I have developed and market an Opal Brightness Kit which consists of a set of natural opals containing three levels of brightness. With this kit, brightness can be judged accurately.

Factors Which Influence Market Value

Before we proceed to detail the identification of opal characteristics, let me summarize them:

Type of Opal: Opal comes in many different types. Some depend on the source of opal, but others are found in more than one location. Common types are solid opal, boulder opal, matrix opal, assembled opal (doublets and triplets), treated or dyed opal, man-made opal, and opal simulants. In addition, type may include the location where the opal is found such as Mexican opal.

Brightness of Fire: The brightness of the fire coming from the stone. To be assessed independently of any other factor.

Base Color: The background color of the stone. This background color may be part of the precious opal, a potch behind the color, or another kind of stone. Background colors include black, semi-black, crystal, semi-crystal, white, orange, gray, brown, boulder black and boulder brown.

Fire Color: The color or combination of colors which are produced when light is diffracted out from the stone. Red, orange, green, and blue are the most common fire colors found in pure form or in combination.

Fire Pattern: The pattern made by the play of color. Patterns are infinite and no two are identical, but they can be generally categorized into pinfire, flashfire, broad flashfire, rare patterns, and harlequins.

Rarity: Some stones are rare or unusual and need to be given special attention. Rarity comes from a unique combination of characteristics. For example, some stones have pictures in them which are particularly attractive.

Cut: The overall shape and quality of cutting. This includes shape, dome, inclusions, and fractures.

Consistency of Fire: The ideal is a stone that shows good fire in all directions as you turn it or pick it up. A stone which shows color only in one direction is called highly directional. Such a stone would have a lower market value. There is, of course, a continuum from non-directional to highly directional.

Conclusion

Using the methodology presented in this book and the objective criteria represented in its photographs you can accurately determine all the characteristics relevant to opal value. By applying these characteristics to the valuing guide developed in Chapter 10, you can produce an accurate estimate of market value.

At times, and perhaps this is one of them, you may feel that this subject is much too complex. There are so many important characteristics and so many subtle variations that it is hard to keep them all in mind. I agree. That is why I have developed this methodology. It unscrambles the computer program in my mind to give you all the steps I went through subconsciously to come up with *X* per carat. Just work systematically through the steps each time and you will succeed.

The opal is a stone of rare and unique beauty. I find it the most enjoyable gem to work with. It has beauty, but it also has infinite variety. It is this variety that makes opal fascinating and valuing opals such a challenge. So let's get started in exploring this wonderful gem.

Review

1.	While each opal is unique, there are some basic characteristics which can be used to determine an opal's market value.

2.	These characteristics are, more or less in order of importance, type, brightness of fire, base color, fire color, fire pattern, rarity, cut and consistency of fire.

3.	This book offers a basic step-by-step methodology for valuing opals using this characteristics approach.

4.	The opal terminology presented in this chapter is a compilation of common usage among opal experts.

5.	To add precision to the definitions of terms, this book contains photographs which provide visual and reproducible criteria for judging these characteristics.

Chapter 2

Equipment Needed

The equipment needed to identify and value an opal is relatively simple but very important. You will need a light source, a carat scale, calipers, a loupe and, of course, this book and my Opal Brightness Kit.

Lighting

Light is the most important ingredient in consistent identification of the characteristics relevant to value and one to which you must pay particular attention. In order to consistently evaluate opals you must do the evaluation in a room with general subdued indirect sunlight and *little or no fluorescent lightning*. Use a single source of light to supplement this background lighting. My system is set up to do identification and valuing using an inexpensive desk lamp available at discount stores for about $10.00. (See Photograph 2-1.) It is important that the lamp have an opaque shade. The bulb used is a common frosted white bulb of 100 watts. This light may not be perfectly color balanced, but it produces consistent grading at minimal cost.

> **Controlled lighting is essential.**

My friends in Lightning Ridge object to this lighting. As Len Cram says, "No dealer worth his salt values Lightning Ridge Black Opal with artificial light." They use indirect sunlight in a room with a northern (southern in our hemisphere) exposure. They view the stone with the light coming over their shoulder. I agree in principle with this objection. The type of light can have a substantial influence on the look of a stone. Indirect sunlight gives the most accurate overall impression of the opal. The problem is that my indirect sunlight and yours will not necessarily be the same. The construction of the building and its orientation to the sun will change the amount of indirect sunlight you have available. So will the weather. The Lightning Ridge Miners Association Opal Advisory Service does not sit when the sky is cloudy because of lack of light.[4] Time of day will influence the result in indirect sunlight. In Australia, opal is only sold between 10 a.m. and 4 p.m. Anyone with experience in Australia and the United States will tell you that opal looks brighter in Australia. Maybe it's the hole in the ozone layer down there. Even differences in latitude in the United States can make a difference. A sapphire dealer from Australia tells me that certain colors of sapphires will not sell in some parts of the United States but will in other parts because of the differences in the way a stone looks in sunlight. Certainly the same is true for opal.

My goal is to produce a grading methodology for opal that can be used anywhere in the United States or the rest of the world at any time and produce consistent and accurate results. Natural indirect sunlight may be best, but it cannot be controlled so that each evaluator is using the same light. Fancy sunlight balanced bulbs may be more natural but they are expensive. I have tried several and found they did not produce results that differed significantly from a simple inexpensive 100 watt frosted bulb. The purpose of choosing this combination of opaque lamp and frosted white 100 watt bulb is to have every evaluator work under identical conditions.

Positioning of the lamp is also important to consistent grading. Set the lamp up so that the bottom of the shade is approximately 20 inches from the surface where the opal is to be judged. Sit or stand so that your eyes are even with the bottom of the shade and looking straight down from the shade to the opal.

---

[4]The Opal Advisory Service consists of six or more miners and dealers who analyze member's opals and estimate their market price.

> ## Every evaluator should work under identical circumstances.

Opal is typically evaluated on a black background. You will need a non-reflecting black surface such as a cloth or construction paper. Shiny paper gives a false impression. You will also want a pure white non-reflecting surface such as a piece of bond paper. The third surface used is your hand.

Photograph 2-1   *Bobbi Downing*
Equipment used for
Opal Evaluation

Opal Brightness Kit

The Opal Brightness Kit consists of a series of natural opals. These stones provide a base against which to judge the brightness of an opal. The kit contains natural stones in three different levels of brightness which I have constructed and calibrated against a master set of opals. Without such a kit it is more difficult to perform a valuation correctly because the criteria for brightness cannot be shown or described accurately with words or photographs. You need these stones to obtain an accurate evaluation. While evaluation can be successful without the Kit, it will be less accurate and replicable. The ideal in opal evaluation is to have independent evaluators separated by time and distance describe a specific opal in identical terms. This is impossible without the Kit. The use of the Kit will be explained in Chapter 6.[5]

---

[5]The Opal Brightness Kit is available through Majestic Opal, Inc., P. O. Box 1348, Estes Park, CO 80517-1348, (800) 468-0324.

Other Equipment

Most opals are sold by weight. Thus, it is necessary to have an accurate scale available. Opals are weighed in carats with an accuracy of two decimal places (0.00 cts). Any scale which will weigh to this accuracy is acceptable. Opals are measured in millimeters. Simple calipers are available for a few dollars. A ten-power (10 X) loupe is also essential to help you see the surface and into the stone.

This is all the equipment you need to identify most opals. There will be some opals which cannot be determined to be natural or synthetic without advanced testing methods requiring a very well equipped laboratory such as GIA maintains. Such difficult cases, which fortunately are fairly rare, may have to be referred to such a laboratory.

Now that we are equipped, let's get started.

Review

1.   In order to generate consistent grading of opals it is necessary for all graders to use the same lighting.

2.   The standard light I have adopted is an inexpensive desk lamp with an opaque shade and a frosted white 100 watt bulb.

3.   Position the light 20 inches above the surface of a table. View the opal with your eye at the level of the shade and directly over the opal.

4.   Brightness cannot be accurately judged without the Opal Brightness Kit.

5.   Other equipment needs are a carat scale accurate to 0.00 carats, calipers in millimeters, and a 10X loupe.

Chapter 3

Identifying Type

There are seven main types of opal and opal substitutes. Within each of these main types are various sub types. By far the most common type of opal is a natural solid stone. The next most common is a triplet. Doublets are less common but gaining more acceptance in the market. Boulder opals are still fairly rare but they are growing rapidly in popularity. The other types, including synthetics and simulants, are still quite rare. While most opal you see in the market is solid opal, one must be careful to correctly determine type, as an error here can substantially affect value. Listed below are the definitions of each basic type.

Types of Opal

Following the definitions I will discuss how to identify each type and its important sub types.

Solid Opal: The vast majority of all opals are solid. A solid opal is completely opal with no non-opal material attached. However, inclusions and a small amount of the parent material such as the sandstone or clay in which the opal is found are allowed. A solid opal may be all precious opal or may be a combination of precious opal and potch. Precious opal is any opal that exhibits a play of color(s) in a distinct pattern. The color is generated from a light phenomena called diffraction. Potch is any opal which does not

Natural Solid Opals

Photograph 3-1   Len Cram

Solid Opal: *Note the combination of precious opal
and potch, as well as the brown clay
in which the opal is found.*

Photograph 3-2   Len Cram

Solid Opal: *Note the black potch in the center of this
stone. This is one way black opal is formed.*

Boulder Opals

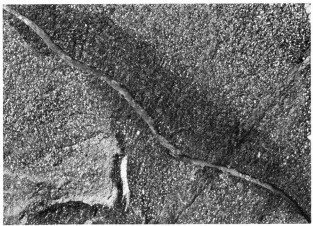

Photograph 3-3   *Len Cram*

Boulder Opal: *Seam of precious opal in ironstone from Queensland. Stone would be cut to expose the line of color, leaving a brown ironstone background.*

Photograph 3-4   *Len Cram*

Yowah Opal: *A mixture of opal and ironstone found in Queensland. A type of boulder matrix opal.*

exhibit a play of color. (See Photographs 3-1 and 3-2.) Notice that Photograph 3-2 shows a black potch inclusion. Such a stone could produce a solid black opal.

Boulder Opal: A seam or patches of solid opal still attached to the parent rock in which the opal is found. The parent material is usually ironstone, but there are many other sources of boulder opal with different parent rocks such as quartzite, rhyolite and basalt. Photograph 3-3 shows a seam of precious opal formed in brown ironstone which is typical of the boulder opal found in Queensland, Australia. It is the most common form of boulder opal found in the market. A different type of boulder opal is presented in Photograph 3-4. The seams are all mixed through the ironstone and cut to show these unique seam patterns. When these seams are very small and completely mixed with the ironstone, the material from Queensland, Australia is referred to as matrix opal. However, to avoid confusion with the matrix opal found in the Andamooka area, I prefer to call this type *Boulder Matrix*.

Matrix Opal: Matrix opal is opal mixed through a parent rock rather than in seams or patches. The three main parent rocks are quartzite, ironstone and basalt. Photograph 3-6 shows the most common type of matrix found in the market. This is matrix opal found in Andamooka, Australia and has been dyed (treated with sugar and acid) to give it a black background.

Treated (Dyed) Opal: A naturally light or clear opal that has been dyed to make it have a dark background. The purpose of dying is to make the stone look similar to a natural black opal, thus increasing its attractiveness and value. (See Photograph 3-6.) The most common treated opal is the Andamooka matrix opal pictured here, but hydrophane opals from Mexico and Brazil have also been successfully treated to dye them black.

Assembled Opal: Opal that has been glued together. A two part stone is called a *doublet*. The back of a doublet may be common opal or any other material. A three part stone is called a *triplet*. It can have almost any material under a thin line of opal. It is topped with a clear material of quartz crystal or glass. (See Photograph 3-7.)

Man-Made Opal: Opal grown in a laboratory. The most common man-made opal is created by *Gilson* in Switzerland. Usually it is a solid opal but it may be made into a doublet or triplet. The synthetic Gilsons shown in Photograph 3-5 are solids and triplets.

Opal Simulants: Non-opal materials produced by man to simulate natural opals. They come in wide varieties. Some are obvious while others are such good copies that experts can be fooled. *Slocum Stone* is one type produced in the United States. A soft plastic simulate, sometimes called *Opalite*, is currently being marketed in Hong Kong. In Photograph 3-5 the stones labeled "Syn. Opal Plastic" are such stones.

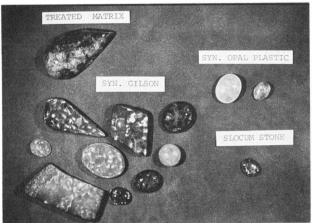

Photograph 3-5   Rudy G. Weber
Synthetics, Simulants, and Dyed Opal

Determining The Type of Opal

The following step-by-step procedure will allow you to determine the type of opal you are examining; at least in most cases. There are always a few difficult exceptions. I will give you as many clues as I can to keep these exceptions to a minimum. Identifying type is difficult to explain and, unfortunately, a bit boring compared to looking at the beauty of the stone. Still, it is absolutely essential as value rests heavily on type.

Solid or Assembled: Is the stone a work of nature or did man put it together? In most cases this is easy to determine. First, holding the stone under your evaluation lamp, look at it from the top, sides, and bottom. Does it appear to be all opal? A stone may be all opal yet still have different colors of stone contained in it. (See

Photograph 3-1 and 3-2.) Sometimes these different colors swirl around; sometimes they lie in very straight lines. If the opal has a play of color throughout the stone, it is almost certainly a solid stone. Many opals consist of a layer of precious opal naturally appearing in common opal. If the stone is all opal and the precious opal is on top of a band of common opal, the stone may be natural or it could be a doublet.

Looking at the stone from the top, is the common opal white or fairly clear? If the answer is yes, then the stone is probably a solid opal. This is because assembled stones (doublets and triplets) are made to look dark from the top to simulate natural black opals. If the stone looks white from the side but dark from the top, it *may* be a doublet. An opal with a line of color on top of a gray or black potch may be natural or a doublet. A line of precious opal through the black potch in Photograph 3-2 could produce a natural black opal even though the surrounding potch is gray.[6]

In all cases where there is the slightest suspicion that the stone is assembled, it should be checked carefully. The method of checking will be explained shortly.

Boulder Opal: Some stones have opal formed with ironstone or other matrix. Such stones are called boulder opal. This is because the ironstone material is typically found in large boulders with the opal mixed through the ironstone. If the opal is mixed irregularly with the ironstone as in Photograph 3-4, it is undoubtedly a natural boulder opal. However, many boulder opals have a thin line of solid opal on top of a thick band of ironstone as in Photograph 3-3. Such stones may be natural or assembled. Many natural boulder opals have what is called a clean face. That is, they do not show any ironstone on the surface of the finished stone. These are the most prized boulder opals. Increasingly, boulder opals with ironstone inclusions in the face of the stone are found in the market. While such stones are less valued, they are gaining popularity. If any ironstone appears on the top of the stone, it is almost certain to be a natural boulder opal. A line of opal that does not have some ironstone mixed with the opal on the top of the stone may be a natural boulder or a boulder doublet, even if it has an irregular, almost carved, surface. Some boulder doublets are very clever and

---

[6]An example of a natural black opal with a white precious opal layer formed below it was shown in *Gems & Gemology*, Spring, 1990, p. 96.

have fooled unsuspecting experts in Australia when they were first introduced to the market some years ago. But once they were known to exist, detection became easy.

> ## Opal on ironstone:
> ## Stone may be natural or a doublet.

Matrix Opal: A combination of opal and a parent rock. There are several types found in the market. The most common is a material found in Andamooka, Australia. This material looks like solid opal except it is somewhat porous. Often the polish on such stones has a satin look. When looked at with a loupe, the surface appears pockmarked with little holes. This surface irregularity is a sure sign of matrix. There is a second characteristic of Andamooka matrix opal. It often has a unique type of pattern found only in matrix opal. The patches of color seem to be made up of sheets of color broken up by tiny crystals or globs of another material. In fact,

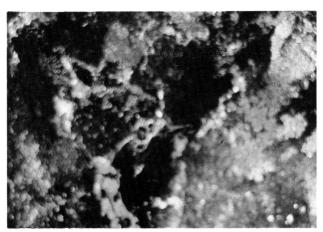

Photograph 3-6   *Len Cram*

Treated (Dyed) Matrix Opal:
Note typical roundish broken pattern.

this is exactly what is happening. (See Photograph 3-6.) The matrix and opal are bound together so that spaces between the precious opal are filled with non-opal material. The edge of each splash of color will appear serrated. It is very difficult to explain this pattern, but once you have seen several stones it will become obvious.

> **Matrix Opal: Stone has a satin finish, looks porous under a loupe, and/or has a distinctive "matrix" pattern.**

The Andamooka matrix opal comes in several background colors. White is most common but seldom seen. This is because most white matrix is dyed black.[7] Andamooka also produces a very attractive translucent to opaque honey-orange base color matrix called "honey matrix." It can be very attractive and is quite rare but not highly valued. There is a rare naturally black matrix found in Andamooka. It is almost impossible to distinguish natural black from dyed matrix. (See Chapter 4.)

Another popular form of matrix opal is boulder matrix. The matrix in this case is ironstone so the finished stone has a medium to dark brown background. The opal may be mixed throughout the ironstone in little spots of color or it may form in small irregular seams or splashes of color. The two most common sources of boulder matrix are Yowah in southern Queensland and Mainside in central Queensland, although there are hundreds of other sources. Each source produces unique patterns of opal and ironstone that are typical of that area. Photograph 3-5 is a typical Yowah pattern.

Another type of matrix opal is commonly found. It is an opal and black basalt found in Honduras. This Honduras opal is easy to identify. First, it has the porous surface typical of matrix opal. Next, it usually contains small flecks of opal spread throughout the stone, giving it the appearance of a pinfire pattern. In addition, the basalt frequently contains small gray inclusions. Finally, it is much lighter in weight than natural opal. On some occasions the satin finish is missing. This may be because the basalt has been treated with a polymer.

---

[7]Grahame Brown, "Treated Andamooka Matrix Opal," *Gems & Gemology*, Summer, 1991, pp. 100-106.

Photograph 3-7   *Tony Dabdoub*
Honduras Matrix *in black basalt*

Doublets and Triplets: There are two types of assembled stones—doublets and triplets. Triplets are simple to identify, doublets may be more challenging.

Photograph 3-8   *Rudy G. Weber*
Opal Triplet: *A three part assembled stone*

To identify a triplet, hold the stone near the opaque shade of your lamp with the side of the stone facing you. Now look through the top of the stone from the side, with the stone between you and the light. A triplet has a clear glass or quartz top which will appear transparent with little or no play of color. If you see this clear top you have at least a doublet and probably a triplet. If the stone appears dark from the top, it is a triplet. Triplets can have any material as the base. Most stones now on the market have clear glass or white ceramic material as their base. The dark color is achieved by painting the back of the opal black. (See Photograph 3-8.)

Triplet: The clear cap is easily recognized from the side. Base may be any color.

Doublets typically consist of a line of opal glued to a common opal backing. The common opal (potch) is typically black opal although gray and white opal are sometimes used. Viewed from the side, most doublets consist of a precious opal top with a perfectly flat seam where the precious opal is glued to the common opal. The top of the stone may be anything from flat to a high dome. Looking at the edge of the stone, examine the contact surface between the precious opal and the common opal using a loupe. You will note several things. The first is the very straightness of the line. Natural opal usually has some irregularity in this line. Precious opal will on occasion penetrate into the common opal in a natural stone. If you have such penetration, you probably have a natural stone. The second thing to look for is a very thin and perfectly straight line of black that may appear right next to the opal. This is the paint and glue used to connect the two pieces. Caution is needed here because natural stones can have a thin black line of common opal sandwiched between the precious opal and a lighter common opal background. These natural stones can usually be distinguished by the slight irregularity of the interface between the black line and the precious opal.

The third characteristic that can be found with a loupe is a difference in texture right where the precious opal and the common opal connect. This is the glue. The glue may not take a polish or it may undercut, producing a slight indention at the joint. Sometimes

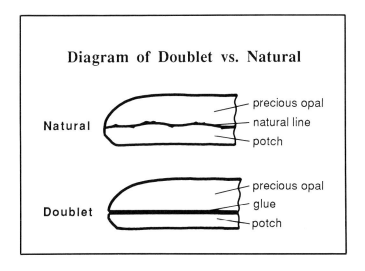

you can feel this edge using the point of a common pin. Any or all of these characteristics will allow you to identify the stone as a doublet. An easier doublet to identify is one that has a backing of another material. If the stone has a backing of black jade, onyx, basanite, or other non-opal material, it is a doublet. There is a second, but very rare type of doublet consisting of a clear cap on top of a layer of solid opal. Looking at the edge of the stone, as you do to find out if it is a triplet, will demonstrate the clear cap.

> **Doublet: Look for the glue line and straight edges between the precious opal and the backing.**

All this works great for stones which are all opal. But boulder doublets take a bit more care. In years past boulder doublets were rarely made. Nowadays they are more common and can be detected fairly easily with a little investigation. The very best boulder opal has a thick seam of precious opal which allows the cutter to produce a smooth low to high dome. However, some natural boulder opals have somewhat wavy lines of color found in the stone. (See Photograph 3-4.) When these natural stones are cut, the contour of the surface is followed. It is essentially carved to expose all the opal. In the old days boulder with an irregular face was of very low value. But nowadays, even these irregular stones can cost several hundred dollars per carat. To simulate these naturally irregular faced boulder opals, cutters have produced doublets with this same carved surface. If you find what appears to be a boulder opal with an irregular carved top but which does not show any ironstone on the top, become suspicious. It is probably natural but it *may* be a doublet.

The technique for producing boulder doublets gives us some clues as to how to detect them. The cutter acquires thin lines of a very bright opal which has replaced clam shells. Such stones are found in Coober Pedy, Australia. These thin lines are carefully carved out on one side, usually the inside of the shell, to remove all traces of sand and other foreign materials. Next this carved surface is painted black. The cutter then carves some ironstone to fit this carved surface as closely as possible. The ironstone and opal are cemented together using epoxy mixed with powdered ironstone. This is so the ironstone and glue combination will fill in any slight gaps between the opal and the ironstone. After the glue is set, the stone is carved and polished on the top just like natural boulder opals. The result is quite convincing, but, take your loupe and look at the interface of the edge between the opal and the ironstone. Usually, natural boulder will have little intrusions of opal into the ironstone and/or intrusions of ironstone into the opal. If you can see such intrusions, you almost certainly have a natural boulder. A second way to detect boulder doublets is to look for the soft glue line between the opal and the ironstone. Use your loupe and a pin point. Probing lightly with the pin point can get a feel of softness (the glue). Third, the loupe may allow you to see the fine ironstone and glue mix between the opal and the ironstone. It takes some careful analysis to separate boulder doublets from natural boulder opals, but it is easy to do once you know what to look for.

Identifying Set Stones

Doublets are readily identified with a little care when they are loose. When set, they are much more difficult to detect. My wife, Bobbi, has a boulder opal ring that she bought set. We were told it is a natural stone and I believe it to be. But, I cannot prove it to my satisfaction because the stone is set in a bezel which obscures all of its edges. The only way to be certain is to take the stone out of the setting which is likely to damage the stone and/or the setting.

Photograph 3-9   Len Cram
This stone, cut and set by the author, is a solid opal.

Most stones are not candidates for being doublets. A white base or crystal base stone is almost certainly not a doublet. A stone which faces black could be a solid, a doublet, or a triplet. If it has a play of color on the back of the stone, it is almost certainly a natural opal. Looking at the side of the set stone, a triplet becomes

> **If you cannot see the edge of any stone set in jewelry, you cannot be absolutely certain it is not a doublet.**

obvious because of the clear cap. Natural black opals can have a black, gray or white potch back, so looking at the back of a set stone and observing black, gray, or white potch does not prove it is natural or a doublet. Frequently you can see the joint between the precious opal and the potch back somewhere in the setting. Examination of the joint with a loupe will show you quickly if the stone is natural or a doublet. In those cases where the edge and bottom cannot be seen, there are still more clues to look for. Sometimes little air bubbles are left between the opal and the glue when making a doublet. These may be seen through the top of the stone using a loupe. Natural inclusions also help identify the stone as a solid. Using all the clues available to you, it is frequently possible to determine that a stone is likely to be natural or likely to be a doublet. Still, there will be a few cases, like Bobbi's ring or my ring, which do not provide enough clues to be certain. When appraising such a stone, I state clearly that it is impossible to determine whether the stone is natural or a doublet. If I believe there is a reasonable chance the stone is a doublet, I give it two values; one as a natural stone and one as a doublet.

The Importance Of Type

The type of opal has a major effect on market value. As a general rule solid opals are more highly valued than matrix opals, with doublets and triplets even farther down the line. Boulder opals, while technically not solid opals, fit into the general price range of solids. Synthetics have become more expensive and often cost more per carat than some solid natural opals. However, they are far less expensive than a natural stone of similar characteristics. Imitations are usually inexpensive.

The Most Important Factors in Value:
- **Type**
- **Base Color**
- **Brightness of Fire**
- **Weight**

While type is of major importance in determining value, it is certainly not the only important factor. The four most important factors are type, brightness of fire, base color, and weight.

You have now identified whether a stone is solid opal or an assembled stone. Before we turn to the other important contributors to value we must do one more thing. It is necessary to determine if the stone is natural, synthetic, a simulant, or dyed. Doublets or triplets are not always made from natural opal. While I have never seen a dyed opal doublet or triplet, I probably will tomorrow. So even if you have determined that a stone is a doublet, you need to go through the discussion in Chapter 4.

Review

1. There are seven main types of opal and opal substitutes; solid opal, boulder opal, matrix opal, treated (dyed) opal, assembled opal (doublets and triplets), man-made (synthetic) opal and opal simulants.

2. Solid opals can be all precious opal or a combination of precious and common (potch) opal.

3. Assembled opals may have backs of common opal, ironstone, jade, or glass, etc.

4. Boulder opal is a natural combination of precious opal and ironstone or other parent rock. Boulder opal consists of a line of precious opal with an ironstone back, while boulder matrix is ironstone with precious opal mixed through it.

5. Treated (dyed) matrix opal has a satin finish, looks porous under a loupe, and/or has a distinctive matrix pattern with a serrated edge to the blocks of fire.

6. Triplets can be easily identified by the clear quartz top to the stone.

7. Doublets can be identified by the straightness of the line of color and the black paint and glue at the joint visible with a loupe.

8. Type is the single most important determinant of opal value.

Photograph 4-1   Manning International

Gilson Synthetic Opal

Photograph 4-2   John Slocum

Slocum Opal Simulant

Chapter 4

Natural, Synthetic, Simulant, Dyed

In the last chapter you determined whether a stone was solid or assembled. For any stone which you found to be solid, and all opal, you must now determine if it is natural, man-made or altered.

Some opals have been created in a laboratory. These synthetic or cultured opals are often difficult to identify without detailed laboratory tests. But there are some clues. First, if the stone has an extraordinarily bright play of color, it may be a synthetic. Next look at the pattern. Most synthetics have an overly regular pattern that looks too consistent to be natural. They also have a roundish globular (snakeskin) pattern such as is shown in Photograph 4-3. From the side, high domed stones will frequently look like the play of color is in columns going from the top to bottom of the stone. Often they feel a little light, too. None of these characteristics prove that the stone is a synthetic, but taken in combination they should make you very suspicious.

Recently, the Gilson Company, which produces most synthetic (or created) opals, has changed its process to produce more natural patterns. The snakeskin pattern is gone. This has made it increasingly difficult to determine when a stone is a synthetic by visual inspection. There is currently a big push to market Gilson opals, so be aware that the stone you are examining may be a synthetic. If the stone is exceptionally bright and has an overly regular pattern, be suspicious.

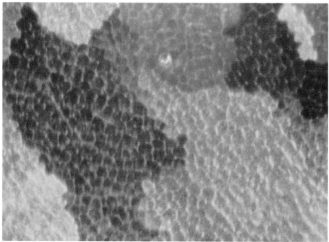

Photograph 4-3   Rudy G. Weber

Gilson Synthetic: Close-up showing the typical snakeskin-like pattern to the fire.

Simulants or Imitations

The distinction between an imitation and a synthetic is one of chemistry. If a man-made stone has the chemical makeup of its natural counterpart, it is called a *synthetic*. If not, it is called an *imitation* or *simulant*.

Imitations of opals have been on the market since the 1920s. At that time, a French company was producing imitation opals which they mounted in costume jewelry. Typically, these imitations show a pinkish background with bluish color play. If viewed from the side, the line of color is at the bottom of the stone. The color line sort of looks like tinfoil, but it is transparent to translucent.[8] The body of these imitations appears to be plastic. To my eye they are obvious fakes, but at least once a month someone shows me a "beautiful opal" that has been in the family for years, or that they just bought at an antique show for a song, which turns out to be one of these fakes.

An imitation which is far more convincing is the *Slocum Stone*. (See Photograph 4-2.) John Slocum's goal was to produce a stone that looked like opal but would wear better. The resulting *Slocum Stone* is available in the rough and in cut stones. It comes in all base colors and in all color plays. Patterns run from large to small. It is a very successful imitation but still there is a look about it that usually makes it obvious that it is not a natural opal. It is hard to describe that characteristic, but it is there in most stones. Still, there are some of his stones which are almost indistinguishable from natural opals to the naked eye. If a stone has a somewhat unnatural look to the fire and from the side it appears that the fire is concentrated in the bottom third of the stone, it may be a *Slocum Stone*. You will become familiar with the look after you have seen a few stones.[9]

Another imitation is a stone made in Hong Kong and sold under the trade name *Opalite*. The first time I saw one of these stones I thought it looked exactly like excellent Mintabie crystal. But then I picked it up. It was light as a feather (specific gravity of 1.20 versus natural opals of 1.99 to 2.25).[10] It was obviously also very soft (about 2.5 on the Mohs scale). It wouldn't stand up in fine jewelry, but is being made into costume jewelry. The play of color comes from little styrene plastic balls in the stone. They produce the same diffraction of light that the silica spheres in opal produce. Because of its natural look, *Opalite* could be passed as natural opal. (See Photograph 3-5.) Although I have yet to know of a case, it is possible that some unscrupulous person could sell it at a high price.

---

[8]See R. Kammerling and R. Weldon, "Microscopic Features of Imitation Phenomenal Gems, Part 2: Plastic Imitations," *Colored Stone*, March/April, 1990, p. 16.

[9]P. Dunn, "Observations on the Slocum Stone," *Gems & Gemology*, 1976, pp. 252-256.

[10]J. Koivula and R. Kammerling, "Opalite: Plastic Imitation Opal with True Play-of-Color," *Gems & Gemology*, Spring, 1989, pp. 30-34.

Photograph 4-4   Rudy G. Weber

Treated (Dyed) Matrix Opal: *Note that
the dye did not penetrate the entire stone.*

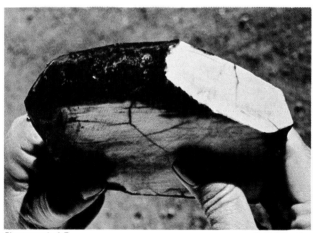

Photograph 4-5   Paul Downing

Treated (Dyed) Matrix Opal: *Note the stark contrast
between the natural white of this stone and the black look
of the dyed area. This chunk has been sawed on the right
and bottom so that the untreated opal is exposed.*

However, the Hong Kong people I have talked to have always identified it as imitation opal. Light weight and softness, as well as its costume jewelry setting, are the distinguishing characteristics of this imitation. You can test hardness by scratching lightly in a non-visible spot with a pin point. *If it scratches, it is not opal.* Also, a hot needle point placed in an inconspicuous spot will melt the plastic.

Dyed Opal

Fortunately most opals cannot be dyed. Opal is simply too impervious. The two exceptions are a particular type of matrix opal from Andamooka, Australia and hydrophane opal.

Dyed matrix is a naturally white stone that is porous. To dye this stone it is first soaked in sugar, then treated with sulfuric acid. The acid causes elemental carbon from the sugar to be deposited in microscopic pores in the stone, dying it black. While some naturally black matrix is found in Andamooka, it is so rare that one can assume that any black matrix opal has been dyed. To prove it, however, is another matter. The dye penetrates only a short distance into the stone. If the stone is broken the interior will be white. (See Photograph 4-4.) In Photograph 4-5, the side and bottom of a large chunk of matrix have been cut away after treatment to expose the white matrix where the treating did not penetrate. Note how the treatment followed the cracks in the stone. Short of breaking a stone, you cannot prove that it is dyed or natural without laboratory tests. However, sometimes you can see the carbon in the pores of the opal using a loupe.[11] Also the matrix has a satin finish rather than the glossy high polish of a solid opal. Finally the matrix opal has a "...typical peppery speckled appearance that is associated with sugar-treated opal from Australia.[12]" It is generally safe to assume that an opal with a matrix pattern and a black base color is dyed, but there are a few exceptions. Short of destroying the stone, you cannot be absolutely certain.

---

[11]Grahame Brown, "Treated Andamooka Matrix Opal," *Gems & Gemology*, Summer, 1991, pp. 100-106.

[12]"Australian Opal Sugar-treated and Coated with Plastic," *Gems & Gemology*, Fall, 1990, p. 236.

There is a second type of dyed opal. It is a hydrophane opal. This opal is very porous and loses the water between the silica spheres easily. Usually the stone turns white as it dries. Hydrophane opal will stick to your tongue because it draws the moisture from it. Hydrophane opal is quite soft and light. This opal can be dyed either by introducing a polymer with dye into it or by smoking it, thus depositing carbon into the pores. If dyed with a polymer, the stone is harder but still lightweight.[13]

There is no easy way to determine if an opal is dyed or smoked hydrophane. Most of the smoked stones come from Mexico so if you see a black Mexican opal it probably will be dyed. While they are very rare, there are reputed to be some natural blacks from Mexico, so you cannot be certain without laboratory tests.[14]

Conclusion

I suspect that this has been a rather discouraging chapter for you. I would like to be able to give you a simple test to prove that a stone is natural, but such a test does not exist. Fortunately, some experience in seeing synthetics and imitations will allow you to identify most of them. Also, synthetics and imitations are still fairly rare so you won't run into this problem frequently. If you are in serious doubt, consult an opal expert or GIA before committing yourself.

Having determined the type of an opal and whether or not it is a natural stone, we can now switch our attention to other characteristics which contribute to the beauty, and thus the value, of an opal.

---

[13]R. Kammerling, J. Koivula, and R. Kane, "Gemstone Enhancement and Its Detection in the 1980s," *Gems & Gemology*, Spring, 1990, p. 35.

[14]"Black Cat's-Eye Opal From Jalisco, Mexico," *Gems & Gemology*, Winter, 1990, p. 304.

Review

1. Synthetic opals have: extraordinarily bright fire, an overly regular pattern with roundish globular edges, and distinctive columns of fire when viewed from the side.

2. Imitation opals are often plastic. In most cases the flashes of color do not look like natural opal.

3. The new imitation opal called *Opalite* is light, soft, and usually set in costume jewelry.

4. Dyed matrix has typical matrix characteristics: satin finish, looks porous, and has a distinctive matrix pattern with serrated edges to the blocks of fire.

5. Dyed hydrophane is very light and softer than natural opal. It may stick to your tongue.

Black Opal

Len Cram

Chapter 5

Base Color

A lady asks, "Do you have any black opals?" We direct her to a display and point out a beautiful black stone with flashes of brilliant red, orange, green and blue. "That's not black." she exclaims, "It has all those colors in it." So the education process begins.

The term *base color* is often confused but it is really very simple. Think about looking at an opal and extinguishing all the fire colors coming from it. What remains is the base color of the stone. Base colors, sometimes called background colors, include black, semi-black, crystal, semi-crystal, white, gray, blue, orange, brown, boulder black and boulder brown. Base color is one of the four primary characteristics which determine an opal's value.

Base color originates in one of three ways. It may be part of the precious opal itself. Alternatively, it may come from an area of common opal (potch) under the line of color. Finally, it may come from the parent stone naturally found associated with the opal. For example, a boulder brown base color results from a water clear line of opal on a natural ironstone boulder back.

The base color of an opal is determined *only* by looking at the top of the stone. With your eye parallel to your lamp, look down at the opal as it rests on your grading table. Notice that it has two color characteristics; the play of fire and a general base color. It is this general base color we wish to determine now.

Definitions of Base Color

In reality, base color is a combination of two things; color and transparency or clarity. The color is what we talked about in the previous paragraphs; the color that is left when there is no fire. That color can be in an opaque stone or, like the purple of amethyst, in a clear stone. Clarity forms in degrees. In opal we divide it into the three levels listed below:

CLARITY

(Degree of Transparency)

- **Crystal** (Transparent)
- **Semi-Crystal** (Translucent)
- **Opaque**

An opal may have any combination of base color and clarity. Thus we see a reddish-orange base color opal from Mexico which is also transparent. This stone would be said to have an orange crystal base color. The combination of two terms tells you about color and clarity. I have a reddish-orange opal in my collection which is opaque. For some reason which I cannot explain, the opal industry adds no modifier for clarity when an opal is opaque. So this opal would be referred to as having a reddish-orange base color, not a reddish-orange opaque base color.

Most base colors can be found in crystal, semi-crystal, and opaque clarities. The exception is white, which can be somewhat translucent but never a true crystal. If a white base stone is opaque, it is referred to in the trade only as white. If it is translucent, it is referred to only as semi-crystal. Actually it would be more accurate to refer to a translucent white as a white semi-crystal to distinguish it from gray semi-crystal. Another word about white base color is appropriate. White stones are seldom white. Most are an off-white but are still called white.

Below is a complete listing of base color definitions. Associated with several of the key definitions are photographs of stones with that base color. This will help you visualize the meaning of the words.

Black Opal: A solid opal which is opaque when viewed from the top of the stone and which has a play of color against a dark background graded as at least number 3 black on the Lightning Ridge Miners Association Tone Scale. The back of the stone may be any color. (Photograph 5-1.)

Black Crystal: A solid opal which is translucent to transparent with play of color which when viewed from the top is graded as at least number 3 black on the Lightning Ridge Miners Association Tone Scale.

Semi-Black: A solid opal which is translucent to opaque when viewed from the top and which has a play of color against a dark gray background corresponding to semi-black on the Lightning Ridge Miners Association Tone Scale. (Photograph 5-2.)

Boulder Black: A natural boulder opal which has a play of color against a dark opaque background graded as at least number 3 black on the Lightning Ridge Miners Association Tone Scale.

Crystal Opal: A solid opal which is transparent as graded by the Clarity Cross showing a play of color and no base color. (Photographs 5-5, 5-8.)

Semi-Crystal: A solid opal which is translucent as graded by the Clarity Cross showing a play of color and a clear to slightly gray or white base color. (Photograph 5-5.)

White Opal: A solid opal which is opaque as graded by the Clarity Cross showing a play of color on a white to off-white base color. (Photograph 5-4.)

Gray Opal: A solid opal which is opaque as graded by the Clarity Cross showing a play of color on a gray base corresponding to the gray tones on the Lightning Ridge Miners Association Tone Scale. (Photograph 5-3.)

Orange Opal: A solid opal which is translucent to opaque as graded by the Clarity Cross showing a play of color on an orange

OPAL BASE COLORS

Photograph 5-1   Len Cram
Black Opal
It is black only if it has a deep
black background when viewed
from the top of the stone.

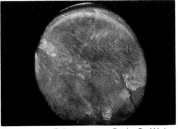

Photograph 5-2   Rudy G. Weber
Semi-Black
The border between black
and semi-black is
frequently vague.

Photograph 5-3   Rudy G. Weber
Gray
A common base color in
both Lightning Ridge and
Mintabie opals.

Photograph 5-4   Rudy G. Weber
White
Commonly from Coober
Pedy. Often off-white.

Photograph 5-5   Rudy G. Weber
Crystal & Semi-Crystal

background. This type of opal would be called red opal or yellow opal depending on the base color.

   Orange Crystal Opal: A solid opal which is transparent as graded by the Clarity Cross showing a play of color on an orange background. This type of opal would be called red crystal or yellow crystal depending on the base color. This has been referred to as fire opal. (Photograph 5-8.)

   Brown Crystal: A solid opal which is transparent as graded by the Clarity Cross showing a play of color on a brown base color. (Photograph 5-7.)

   Jelly Opal: A solid opal which is transparent as graded by the Clarity Cross showing no play of color, but it may show an opalescence without a pattern in the fire. The orange material without a play of color from Mexico is frequently seen in faceted stones, and would be termed orange jelly.

   Blue Opal: A solid opal which can be transparent to opaque with or without a play of color on a blue base color. Terminology should be adjusted depending upon clarity and presence of fire.

Black Opal Criteria

The most valuable of base colors is black.
   The lack of understanding of the term *Black Opal* is widespread indeed, even among opal miners, dealers, and jewelers. In order for a stone to be truly a black, it must have a rich dark black background, as in Photograph 5-1. This would be simple if all opals either had this dark base color or a light one. But nature does not work that way. Base colors come in all shades of gray. (See Photographs 5-2 and 5-3 for examples.) How dark must the base color of a stone be for it to be considered a black? Opinions vary but there is a general tendency in the market to call even light gray stones "black opal" because black opal commands a premium price. Some people consider any stone from Lightning Ridge, Australia a black, but in reality *most* of the stones produced there are *not* black opal by the standards used by the Lightning Ridge Miners Association.

The first time we went to Lightning Ridge we wanted to learn what the experts on the Opal Advisory Service of the Lightning Ridge Miners Association defined as black opal. Ted Priester, Secretary of the Opal Advisory Service, stated there is still a great deal of confusion about what constitutes a black opal, even among the miners. The miners call many stones black when, in fact, the association would not define them as black.

What then does the Lightning Ridge Miners Association consider a black opal? According to the Association, a stone is a black opal only if "...it shows a dense black background when viewed from the top of the stone." The black must come from the opal, not from another material such as the ironstone of boulder opal. Ted says that it does not matter what the stone looks like from the back. A black back does not make the stone a black opal, just as a white or gray back does not preclude it from being a black. Indeed, I have an example of a black opal with a natural white potch back. In between this white base and the color line is a thin line of black potch making the opal have a black base color from the top. Also, I have seen stones that face as deep blacks which had the black in with the color and a light gray back. In black opals, its what's up front that counts.

The most preferred black is one that shows a liquid royal blue that flows over the top of a stone with other colors on a dense black background. This is the best gem black. Old timers speak glowingly of stones they found or have seen by saying "Ah, it had the blue." Such is enough to identify it as something really special. Len Cram, a miner and dealer with many years of experience on the fields in Lightning Ridge, says that he has seen only a couple dozen such stones. "They are out of this world!" he exclaims.

Ted showed us a set of stones which were pure potch (non-precious opal) but which ranged in background color from crystal (water clear—like glass) and white to jet black. (See Photograph 5-6.) Next to the white were a light and a darker gray (termed a gray), then a medium gray (termed a semi-black), and three degrees of black ranging from slate to pure jet black. Each Saturday morning the Lightning Ridge Miners Association offers a grading and valuing service to its members. Each cut stone is compared to these background stones and only those which meet this standard are graded as black opals.

The Gemological Institute of America (GIA) in its *Gem Reference Guide*, part of its Gem Identification and Colored Stone Grading Course, defines black opal as "translucent to opaque with play of color against a black, dark gray, blue, green, brown or other dark body color.[15]"   Thus they are more inclusive than the Lightning Ridge Miners Association, but agree that the base color should

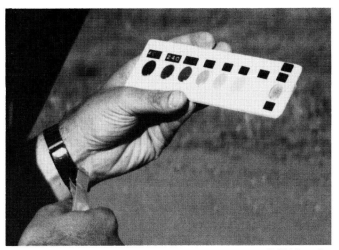

Photograph 5-6   *Bobbi Downing*

Base Color Standard: *Developed by*
The Lightning Ridge Miners Association.

be dark. The GIA definition of black seems to allow boulder opal as a black opal if it is dark. Clearly the Lightning Ridge Miners Association definition does not allow this. To them boulder opals cannot be black. However, there is a difference of opinion on this issue among opal people in Australia. One dealer points out that dark boulder opal is true black opal because there is a thin layer of black potch between the opal and the ironstone matrix. Most refer to boulder opals that face as black opals as "boulder blacks." The GIA definition also accommodates the dark brown based blacks from Nevada and Java.

Recall that there are two different ways an opal can produce the dark base color called black opal. One is when the black base color is included with the fire in the top of a stone. The other is

---

[15]Gemological Institute of America, *Gem Reference Guide*, 1988, p. 164.

when clear opal, called *crystal*, is found on top of a black potch background. This type of opal has sometimes been called a "natural doublet." However, that term has been rejected as inappropriate by the *Australian Gem Trade Association* because of its confusion with doublets and the implication this type of black opal is inferior to the other type. Either of these types would be called black opal by the Lightning Ridge Miners Association's definitions if they face up dark enough. Stones not facing up dark enough are called semi-black by most dealers, the AGIA, GIA and *The Guide*, although the Lightning Ridge Miners Association just call them dark gray. Some stones have a dark base included with the fire but are translucent throughout. Such stones are called black crystal. A black crystal shows a red-orange color in transmitted light. This can be readily seen by shining a penlight through the stone onto a white piece of paper.

Photograph 5-7   *Morris Ratcliffe*
Brown Crystal from Nevada.

    The dark brown referred to in the GIA definition is usually found in the Nevada opal fields. When dense, this dark brown faces as black and would be graded as a black opal. Some Nevada opals are a transparent dark brown as in Photograph 5-7. These would be graded as black crystal. Other Nevada blacks and the Java blacks are so dense that they become opaque and appear black, not brown. An example is the right side of Photograph 5-7. These would be termed black rather than black crystal. While cuttable black opal from Nevada is rare, it does exist, so be on the lookout for this unique material.

The *Gemological Association of Australia* (GAA) and the *Australian Gem Industry Association* (AGIA) provide a separation of black opals into three types; black, semi-black, and black crystal. Their definitions, as presented in the GAA publication *Valuation of Australian Precious Opal*, 1988, are as follows:

> "**DARK OPAL** - This group have a very dark to black body colour.
>
> i.   Semi Black
>
> There has been a lot of conjecture over the dividing lines between gray, semi black and black. When does an "i" colour become "j" colour? Naturally, experts will differ slightly in opinion particularly in border line cases. Border line semi black should appear very dark gray when viewed on a white background, perhaps the darkness of a nimbus cloud. Semi black has risen in popularity recently with the advent of greater supplies due to the Mintabie and more recently the Sheepyard area of Glengarry.
>
> ii.   Black Crystal
>
> As with the light variety, this type has a transparency which allows diffracted colours to be detected below the surface of the gem.
>
> iii.   Black Opal
>
> The trade generally accepts as black those stones that have a very dark appearance. If placed on a white background, view the stone whilst squinting, the gem should appear black. This is the rarest and most valuable category.
>
> As previously explained, boulder can fall into any of the previous categories, the difference being the presence of ironstone on the base of the gem. They are not referred to as natural doublets but rather classified as solid opal."

The Guide also divides dark stones into black, semi-black, and black crystal but their definitions are slightly different, particularly their insistence that a black opal be completely opaque. Here are their definitions:

> **"Black Opal**: Opal with black or very dark background showing play of color. Must be opaque when held up to a light and viewed from the face.

> **Semi-black Opal**: Opal with dark gray or other dark background, semi-translucent and with play of color.

> **Crystal-black Opal**: Opal with dark gray or other dark background, with play of color when viewed in the usual manner, but when held to the light the opal is quite transparent to translucent."

Faced with all these different definitions, what can we do? I have adopted definitions which accommodate all these slightly different perspectives. But we are still faced with a problem.

How dark does a stone need to be to be called a black?

The only visual guide now available is the Lightning Ridge Miners Association criteria stones. Below I have reproduced the background or base color shadings they employ. (Figure 5-1.) If a stone is natural and has a base color at least as dark as #3 black, the Lightning Ridge Miners Association considers it a black opal. I have adopted their criteria here. Boulder opals that have a black base color fitting the Lightning Ridge criteria, I refer to as Boulder Black. Compare this visual criteria with the pictures presented in this chapter. Remember that it is important to look at the base color, not the play of color.

The definitions I have presented earlier in this chapter have integrated the various definitions of black and semi-black. In effect, my definitions combine the essential elements of all the definitions in one consistent and quantifiable set of criteria.

Figure 5-1

Lightning Ridge Miner's Association
Tone Scale

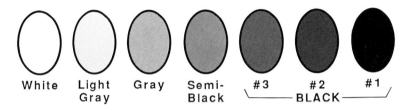

| White | Light Gray | Gray | Semi-Black | #3 | #2 | #1 |

BLACK

Criteria For Crystal and Semi-Crystal

When does a white base stone become sufficiently translucent to be a semi-crystal? Or when is an opal clear enough to be called a crystal? Again we are faced with the lack of a visual criteria for determining dividing lines. Since no visual criteria is available, I have produced my own which I now offer for your consideration.

Figure 5-2

Clarity Cross

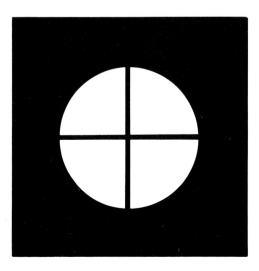

On the preceding page you will see a black square with a white circle containing a cross in its center. I call this a *Clarity Cross*. (Figure 5-2.) It is used to judge the clarity of an opal. The three degrees of clarity used in the opal trade are opaque, translucent, and transparent.

To determine whether a stone is white, semi-crystal, or crystal, place this book on the surface 20" below your lamp open to page 49. Next, place the opal on the edge of the white circle so that half of the stone is on the black and half is on the white. Observe the base color of the opal with your eye even with the shade of your lamp. If the half of the stone on the black appears to have a darker base color than the half on the white, the stone is at least a semi-crystal (or translucent). Then place the opal over the center of the cross. If the cross is visible through the stone, the opal is a crystal (or transparent).

Photograph 5-8   *Morris Ratcliffe*
Orange and Other Base Colors

This criteria works well for most stones. However, there are a few crystal opals that are completely transparent but have such dense play of color that you cannot see the cross. If you have a translucent to transparent stone with very dense fire, you will have to employ some judgment. Hold the stone up so that it is between you and the lamp. If you can see through it easily, classify it as a crystal. If it appears somewhat opaque, classify it as a semi-crystal. Also, if a stone has a somewhat whitish body color, classify it as a semi-crystal. Note also that the thickness of the stone affects the reading on the clarity cross. If a stone is large and thick, it will be more difficult to see the clarity cross and the dark background. You will need to adjust using the transmitted light test discussed above.

It is important to remember that the term crystal refers to the degree of transparency of a stone, not its base color. Thus, a stone which has a black, brown, gray, orange, or blue base color and is highly transparent is still a crystal. Like black crystal there is gray or semi-black crystal. The typical Mexican opal is orange crystal. (See Photograph 5-8.)

The term *fire opal*, commonly used for orange-base transparent opal with no play of color, leads to great confusion in the public. People frequently ask me for fire opal. When shown the Mexican orange crystal they say, "No, I want something with fire in it." What the general public thinks of as "fire opal" is a crystal or semi-crystal from Australia with lots of red play of color (fire).

We need to change the term for the Mexican opal from "fire opal" to "orange opal."

Finally, there is confusion between *jelly* and *crystal*. If there is an attractive play of color and identifiable pattern in a stone, it is crystal. Jelly refers *only to* clear opal with or without opalescence but having no definable pattern.[16] Technically, jelly opal is not precious opal.

Determining Base Color

To determine the base color of a stone, place the stone face up on the page containing the black and gray screenings of the Lightning Ridge Miners Association criteria stones. (Figure 5-1.) Move the stone next to the base color that appears to most closely match it. That is your base color, except if the stone has a base color other than in the white-black continuum. If a stone has no base color (it looks clear like glass) or if it is somewhat translucent, it may be a crystal or semi-crystal. For any stone which shows translucency, perform the clarity cross test described above. Orange, brown, and blue base colors are immediately obvious without reference to a

---

[16]Gemological Institute of America, *Colored Stone Course, Assignment 17*, 1990, p. 12.

color guide, although reference to Photographs 5-7 and 5-8 may be helpful. Using these two criteria, each stone can be uniquely defined as to its base color and clarity. Remember that you are judging the base color only. Do not pay any attention to the color of the fire coming from the stone. (Hard, I know, but you can do it.)

Base Color and Value

There is nothing more spectacular than seeing flashes of reds, greens, and blues set against a rich black background, as seen in Photograph 5-1. Such a combination produces the rarest and most valued of opals, a red on black. The value of such rare stones exceeds the value per carat of most other precious stones and diamonds. *Yes, an opal can be more valuable than a diamond.* After all, it is far more rare. And, in my opinion, far more beautiful.

Semi-blacks follow in value per carat. Crystal opals and boulder opals are next with semi-crystal stones very close. Gray, white, orange and other base colors are less valuable than those listed above. There is very little difference in value per carat for these base colors, other things being equal.

But, as you know, in opals "other things" are never exactly equal. We have already talked about the major effect of brightness of fire on value. Of lesser effect on value are such characteristics as fire color and pattern. We turn our attention to the first of these, fire color, next.

Review

1.   There are two characteristics which make up the term base color; color and clarity.

2.   The term black opal is frequently misunderstood. It should be used only to refer to dark base color stones meeting the criteria of the Lightning Ridge Miners Association Tone Scale.

3.   Base color (tone) is determined with reference to the Lightning Ridge Miners Association Tone Scale.

4. Solid opals and boulder opals are never referred to as "natural doublets."

5. The dark base colors are referred to as black, semi-black and gray. In addition there are red, orange, yellow, blue, green, and brown base colors.

6. Clarity refers to the degree to which you can see through an opal. The range is from transparent (referred to as crystal), through translucent (referred to as semi-crystal), to opaque (with no special terminology).

7. Clarity can be measured by using the Clarity Cross.

8. Definitions of an opal's base color have been modified slightly to make clear the degree of clarity as well as base color being referred to.

Brilliant Flashes of Fire
Make Opal Unique

Len Cram

Chapter 6

Brightness of Fire

When I think of opal, I think of bright flashes of color bouncing up at me, changing as I move the stone in my hand. They are *mesmerizing*. These flashes of color are what set precious opal apart from any other gemstone. The brightness of these flashes differs from stone to stone and even from place to place in the same stone. Opals with faint flashes of color are considered precious opal, but the really brilliant flashes are what determine that the opal is a top gem.

The brightness of the fire coming out of an opal is one of the most important contributors to its beauty and value. It is also the most difficult characteristic to judge consistently. One reason for this is that people cannot keep the degree of brightness of a stone accurately in their mind over time. There is a tendency to elevate the brightness of the stone the person is currently examining relative to others seen previously. I don't know why this is the case, but it is. The other reason is that brilliance is seriously affected by the light under which the opal is viewed. That is why some opal sellers use those little high power lamps. They make an opal appear brighter than it would appear in natural sunlight, thus giving the impression that the stone is of greater brightness than it is, implying it has greater market value. In Chapter 2 we discussed the need for a consistent lighting source in evaluating an opal. This is most important when judging brightness.

Several dealers have their own stones which they carry with them on buying trips. They use these stones to judge brightness under differing conditions. They compare their stones to those being offered to them. Since they know their stones, they can judge how the available light affects the opal being offered for sale. Each of us could do the same. The problem is that each of us would use a different standard for brightness.

In order to accurately grade the brightness of an opal, it is necessary to have a consistent light source and a set of stones to compare to the one you are grading.

Brightness Standard

In an effort to produce a consistent brightness standard, the American Opal Society (AOS) produced an evaluation kit which contained five stones of differing degrees of brightness. Unfortunately, these kits are no longer available. To solve this problem I have produced my own *Opal Brightness Kit* which contains opals consistently graded for brightness. (Photograph 6-1.) Following the

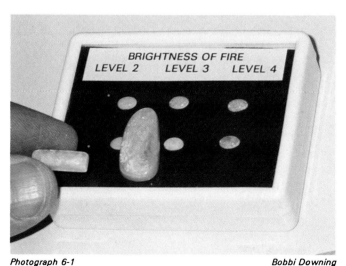

Photograph 6-1   *Bobbi Downing*
Opal Brightness Kit

AOS, I have employed five (5) levels of brightness (they called it intensity) which are represented in the kit by three levels. I leave the lowest and highest levels out for economy and because if a stone is brighter than the highest level shown, Level 4, it fits into the brightness Level 5. You do not need the stone to determine that.[17]

Each Opal Brightness Kit contains carefully selected opals which match the brightness of similar opals in a master kit. In this

Brightness Table

Brightness Level	Name	Description
1	Faint	Shows play of color only under direct sunlight and even then the fire is faint.
2	Dull	Shows some color under low light but even under indirect sunlight or the grading lamp the fire is dull.
3	Bright	Shows fair color under low light and very nice fire under indirect sunlight or the grading lamp.
4	Very Bright	Shows good color under low light and sharp crisp color under indirect sunlight or the grading lamp.
5	Brilliant	Shows exceptionally bright crisp color under indirect sunlight or the grading lamp and often shows even brighter in subdued light.

way, each kit will exhibit the same brightness under your grading light as it does under mine. Furthermore, by selecting stones under this same light your Opal Brightness Kit will match any other I have produced. This allows each grader to produce an accurate grading

---

[17]The **Opal Brightness Kit** is available from Majestic Opal, Inc., P. O. Box 1348, Estes Park, CO 80517-1348, (800) 468-0324.

OPAL BRIGHTNESS LEVELS

Photograph 6-2   Rudy G. Weber
Level 1 - Faint

Photograph 6-3   Rudy G. Weber
Level 2 - Dull

Photograph 6-4   Rudy G. Weber
Level 3 - Bright

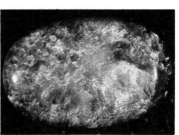

Photograph 6-5   Rudy G. Weber
Level 4 - Very Bright

Photograph 6-6   Rudy G. Weber
Level 5 - Brilliant

of the brightness of any opal. It should be possible to send the opal to any other grader with an Opal Brightness Kit and obtain the same brightness level. You would be able to call on any dealer who has an Opal Brightness Kit, have him send you an opal of brightness Level 3 and receive an opal of a brightness equal to the Level 3 stones in your kit. The goal is to make brightness grading equivalent to color grading in diamonds.

> **Brightness is the amount of light coming back from the opal.**

On the preceding page you will see a series of five pictures which represent these five levels of brightness. (See Photographs 6-2 through 6-6.) I term these levels as faint (1), dull (2), bright (3), very bright (4), and brilliant (5). It is easy to see the difference between these stones in the pictures. It is tempting to use these pictures as a guide for brightness. However, a grading done using the pictures will not be as accurate as one using my Opal Brightness Kit. The pictures may overstate or understate brightness relative to the kit, depending on how your eyes perceive these colors. Recall that brightness is the amount of light coming back at you, not the color.

Judging Brightness

To judge brightness, set your kit on the working surface 20" below your lamp. With your eye at lamp level, place the opal to be graded on the glass next to the example stones. Make sure the printing on the kit is right side up. Turn your stone to observe the flashes of color as the light hits it from various directions. Pick up the stone and hold it at various angles to the light. The object is to get an impression of the general brightness of this opal. Compare its overall brightness to the overall brightness of the kit stones, matching the stone with the equivalent kit stone. Leave the kit face up on the table and look down on it from above the light to get an accurate picture of the brightness levels of the stones in the kit. The Level 4 stone should be to your right. At other angles a particular stone in your kit may appear to be a different brightness level. Do not use any brightness level but the level seen as you look down on the kit from above with Level 4 to the right.

Remember that you wish to judge the overall brightness of the stone. Frequently there will be a small area that has brighter or duller fire than the rest of the stone. Do not base your judgment of brightness on these small areas. It is the overall impression that is essential.

Next move the stone away from the light of your lamp. Note how the brightness (and sometimes the color) of the fire changes. Some stones look fairly bright under the lamp but lose a lot of brightness when removed from the light. These should be graded one brightness level lower if the brightness change is dramatic. Other stones may actually look brighter under lower light. These opals are true prizes and should be upgraded in brightness one level. I think the reason for this positive change is that these stones diffract light back so much that they look somewhat washed out under the lamp. There is so much light coming to your eye that your eye cannot absorb it all and the opal starts to look like white light. It is like an overexposed color picture. Under lower light, your eye can absorb the colors and distinguish them so the stone appears brighter. Such stones are sometimes called "night stones."

One of our customers tests all his stones by taking them from the light and placing them under the table. This is a good way to perform the test. However you do the test, be aware of the general light in the room. If it is fluorescent it will show blues better and reds less unless the bulbs are color compensated to simulate natural light. The level of background light will also affect the test. When you do grading in a controlled situation such as your work space, you will get used to how good stones react as you move them out of the 100 watt grading light. However, when you have no control of the light such as when you attend a gem show, it may be helpful to take the Opal Brightness Kit, or a couple of opals you know well, along with you to judge the effect of the lighting on the opals.

Brightness Is Most Important

The brightness of the fire coming back from an opal is one of the four primary factors which determine its value, the other three being type, base color, and weight. There is no other gemstone which can rival the beauty of a truly brilliant opal. The flashes of brilliant fire in top gems I have seen come to mind readily. But I wouldn't trust myself to say which stone was brighter unless I could compare them to each other or to my Opal Brightness Kit, even after 28 years of experience. You shouldn't trust your memory either.

Now that you have learned about base color and brightness, let us turn our attention to other factors which affect value.

Review

1. The brightness of the fire bouncing back from an opal is a major determinant of its value, the brighter the better.

2. Lighting has a major effect on the appearance of brightness of the stone. You need to control light or otherwise adjust to differing lighting conditions using a control such as the Opal Brightness Kit.

3. The Opal Brightness Kit provides a set of stones which exhibit different levels of brightness. Each kit is calibrated against a master kit to provide a consistent measure of brightness.

4. Comparing the opal to be valued to the Opal Brightness Kit allows you to determine its brightness level.

5. Moving the opal away from the light gives you an idea of how well the brightness holds as lighting changes. A truly exceptional opal is one that is brilliant (Level 5 brightness) in and out of the grading light.

Fire Comes in All the
Colors of the Rainbow

Rudy G. Weber

Chapter 7

Fire Color

I love all opals, but I am especially fond of bright, broad flashes of reds, particularly if they are mixed with blues and a bit of orange and green as the stones move. My wife loves the greens and blues with a bit of orange. Between us, we run the gambit of color preferences. The market reflects our preferences. The reds are most preferred while green-blue fire is somewhat less preferred. This preference is changing in the United States. It used to be that green-blues were much less preferred and had a much lower market value. Nowadays the green-blue crystals are almost as valued as red crystal. In black opals red is quite a bit more valuable than green-blues. Whatever your preferences, there is a combination of fire colors for you.

Fire color is the term for the color flashing out of the opal and caused by the optical phenomena called diffraction.[18] Since these colors are produced by light, they can be all the colors of the rainbow.

There is an interesting physical phenomena in fire color. Some splashes of fire change color as you move the opal. In effect, you are moving up and down the color spectrum as the angle of light

---

[18]For an explanation of the source of opal's fire and how it differs from other light phenomena in gemstones, see Emmanuel Fritsch and George Rossman, "An Update on Color in Gems. Part 3: Colors Caused By Band Gaps and Physical Phenomena," *Gems & Gemology*, Summer, 1988, pp. 81-102.

Typical Fire Color Combinations

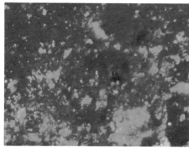

Blue Only

Photograph 7-1   *Rudy G. Weber*

Blue-Green

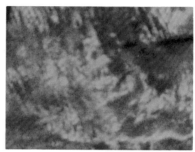

Photograph 7-2   *Rudy G. Weber*

Green-Blue

Photograph 7-3   *Len Cram*

Orange-Green

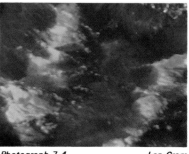

Photograph 7-4   *Len Cram*

Typical Fire Color Combinations

Orange-Red

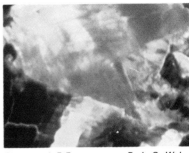

Photograph 7-5   Rudy G. Weber

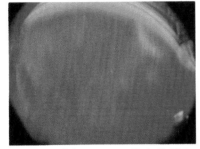

Red Only

Photograph 7-6   Rudy G. Weber

Multicolor

Photograph 7-7   Len Cram

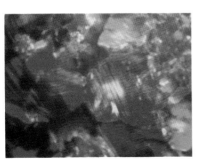

Red Multicolor

Photograph 7-8   Rudy G. Weber

changes. Other splashes of fire keep the same color but move across the surface. These color changes are what make opal so fascinating.

Dominant Color

In order to describe the range of fire colors in an opal, it is traditional to refer first to the most dominant color. The second most dominant color is then mentioned: If there are more than two colors that appear prominently in the stone, the stone is referred to as multicolor. If there is one dominant color along with several supporting colors, the stone is referred to by that dominant color and multicolor. Thus, a stone which has a dominant red play of color and several other supporting colors would be called a "Red Multicolor." A stone showing a predominance of green with supporting blue would be called a "Green-Blue" while one in which the blue dominates over the green would be referred to as "Blue-Green."

Table 7-1
Typical Fire Color Combinations

Color Combination	Photographs
Blue Only	7-1
Blue-Green	7-2
Green-Blue	7-3
Orange-Green	7-4
Orange-Red	7-5
Red Only	7-6
Multicolor	7-7
Red Multicolor	7-8

On the preceding pages I present a series of photographs that represent the most common combinations of play of color and which are summarized in Table 7-1. To determine the fire color of your stone, compare it to these photographs. Hold the stone 20" under your lamp and move it in your fingers. As you do, notice which color dominates and which colors provide strong support. Here you will need a little judgment. You will need to decide if a color should be counted. The criteria I use is whether the color adds substantially to the look of the stone. If it does, it counts as a color. But if it shows weakly and only from certain angles, do not count it. The tendency is to count too many colors. The fire must add significantly to the look of the stone.

The Multicolor Rule

An opal is considered to be a multicolor stone when it has at least *three* strong fire colors. Usually one of these colors will dominate. If so, the stone is referred to first by the dominant color, then by multicolor. Thus a stone which shows a dominant orange play of color with strong green and blue supporting it would be referred to as an "Orange Multicolor." Sometimes it is helpful to go a little further. Suppose, as in Photograph 7-4, that a stone has two dominant colors and several strong supporting colors. It may then be referred to as, in this case, an "Orange-Green or an Orange-Green Multicolor." Usually in such cases the term multicolor is dropped but it is more descriptive than just orange-green, since there are other colors present.

The opposite case is when there is only one dominant color of fire and no supporting fire colors. The opal is then referred to by only that color. For example, the first stone pictured in this chapter (Photograph 7-1) shows only blue fire except for a couple of red and green spots which are not sufficient to add to the look of the stone. Thus, this stone is referred to as having only a blue play of color.

The question of dominance of color can be a matter of perception and judgment. For example, I consider Photograph 7-2 as a stone in which the blue fire dominates over the green. Hence, I call it a blue-green. Photograph 7-3 has more green and the green provides the dominant pattern so I call it a green-blue. Photograph 7-7, listed as Multicolor, is the closest I can come to a stone which shows several different fire colors but none is dominant. However, I expect that most in the trade would call this a Red Multicolor.

Red Multicolor is considered the most valuable of all fire colors. When it is combined with a blue fire on a black background, it is truly exceptional. The lovely stone in Photograph 7-8 is an outstanding example of this prized and rare color. You will be lucky to see one or two stones of this quality in a lifetime.

Judging Fire Color

The stones photographed here provide a nice visual criteria for determining the fire color of your stone. Comparing your stone to these pictures, you should have no difficulty characterizing its fire color. Be careful, however, as there is a tendency to count too many colors. Remember, the color must add significantly to the look of the stone to be counted.

Review

1. To characterize the fire colors found in an opal, the most dominant color is referred to first. Other colors which contribute significantly to the look of the stone are added. Thus, an opal which shows a dominant orange and supporting red would be referred to as having orange-red fire color.

2. An opal would be considered a multicolor stone *only* if it has at least *three* strong fire colors.

3. Be careful not to count too many colors. Only those colors which add significantly to the look of the stone should be counted.

Chapter 8

Fire Pattern

You might wonder why a chapter on the patterns in opal is so far back in this book. In spite of all the attention paid to pattern, it, like fire color, has far less influence on price than commonly believed. Most opals (at least 90%) have a pattern that fits into the *flashfire* or *broad flashfire* categories. Since there is very little difference in value for these patterns, the value of most stones is unaffected by pattern. The patterns which can significantly affect value are the unusual ones like harlequin and other rare patterns. So, we have a strange contradiction. The thing that makes each opal so unique, its pattern, usually is not a major contributor to its value.

The fire pattern is the pattern made by the play of color in the stone. Patterns are infinitely variable and no two are ever exactly alike. However, they can be generally categorized.

Patterns Defined

One of the favorite games that opal people play is "Name That Pattern." For whatever reason, people just love to make up names. *Exploding fire. Fireworks. Snakeskin. Rainbow. Peacock.* Names are as fanciful and unique as the individual doing the naming. Barrie O'Leary's book, *A Field Guide to Australian Opals* is a good example of this phenomena. Most of these names are unique to the individual doing the naming. Others are more commonly used, but their meaning differs from person to person.

Photograph 8-1   *Rudy G. Weber*

Pinfire: *Small pinpoint circles of fire.*

Photograph 8-2   *Len Cram*

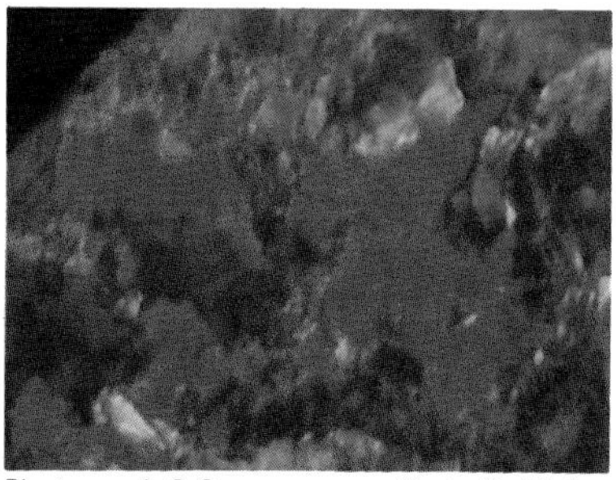

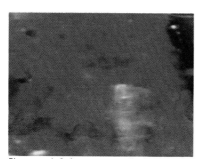

Photograph 8-3   *Rudy G. Weber*

Flashfire: *Larger irregular splashes of fire. No individual splash covers a large percentage of the stone.*

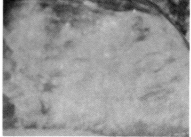

Photograph 8-4   *Rudy G. Weber*

Photograph 8-5   *Rudy G. Weber*

Broadflash: *Sheets of color covering a large portion of the opal's surface.*

While many names are fanciful and unique to the individual doing the naming, there are a set of commonly accepted names for fire patterns. These names are defined below:

Pinfire: Small pinpoint circles of fire. When viewed from the side, this pattern often looks like the side of a stack of pins, while the top view looks like the points of those pins, hence the name. The side view is called *columnar fire*. (See Photograph 8-1.)

Flashfire: Larger areas of fire, usually irregular in shape. The splashes of fire can be fairly large but no one area would cover more than 50% of the surface of the opal.[19] (See Photographs 8-2 and 8-3.)

Broad Flashfire: Sheets of color usually covering a large section or all of the stone's surface.[20] (See Photographs 8-4 and 8-5.)

Rolling Flashfire: Sheets of color which roll across the surface of the stone as it is moved. This type of pattern is almost impossible to photograph but is highly prized.

Harlequin: Square or angular blocks of fire set closely together. True harlequins, like those in Photographs 8-6 and 8-7, are rare indeed. Rare and unusual patterns that are not regular are also especially valued but not true harlequins.

These patterns are illustrated in Photographs 8-1 to 8-6. True *Pinfire* is even more regular and round than in Photograph 8-1. *Flashfire* is the most common pattern. There is a continuum of sizes of color from very small like pinfire to a single large sheet of fire which constitute broad flashfire. As always, there will be some stones which are at the borders. The bright red splashes of color shown in Photograph 8-4 clearly dominate this stone. It is not necessary that a patch of color cover the entire surface of the stone

---

[19]GIA lumps flashfire and broad flashfire into one category called broadflash. *Colored Stone Grading*, Lesson 17, p. 13.

[20]See footnote 3.

Photograph 8-6   Rudy G. Weber
Harlequin Closeup

Photograph 8-7   Len Cram
Beautiful Harlequin Pattern

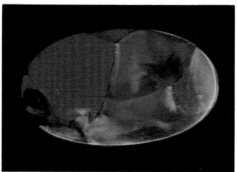

Photograph 8-8   Rudy G. Weber
Flagstone Harlequin

before the opal is termed a broad flashfire pattern. If flashes of color are in sheets that are large relative to the surface area of the stone, each one covering say 40 to 50% of the area, the stone would be said to have a broad flashfire pattern.

Rolling Flashfire: This is fairly rare. The term does not refer to one single sheet of fire which shows in some orientations but not in others. Rather, it refers to one or several chunks of color which seem to float or roll over the surface of the stone as you move it. It is almost as if the pattern moves across the stone as the opal is moved.

Harlequin Pattern

The most frequently misunderstood and misused term in fire patterns is *Harlequin*. According to *Webster's College Dictionary*, the term comes from the costume of the buffoon in a "*commedia dell'arte*" usually masked, dressed in multicolored, diamond-patterned tights. . Used as an adjective it means "having a pattern of brightly colored diamond shapes." In opal it is used for a rare regular square pattern of colors. (See Photograph 8-6 and 8-7.) The strictest definition allows only these regular squares; however, terminology has been broadened over the years. GIA defines a harlequin as "broad, angular, close-set patches of color." (*Gem Reference Guide*.) O'Leary, in his book *A Field Guide to Australian Opals* (p. 23), defines the term as "a regular mosaic-like (fire) pattern in rounded, angular, or roughly square patches of about equal size." Thus he allows roundish patterns as well. The problem is that when you allow for "roundish" patterns you have no real guideline any more. The inevitable end result is that people term all sorts of stones as harlequin. In O'Leary's book, he calls many stones harlequins that do not meet his own definition, and his definition is not generally accepted by the opal trade. His terms, like floral harlequin, are not true harlequin patterns by the commonly accepted definitions of the term because they are not square or angular.

The two stones shown in Photographs 8-6 and 8-7 have true harlequin patterns. There is another rare pattern called a *Flagstone Harlequin* which contains angular patches of color that are of different shapes, but all fit together perfectly as would a flagstone walkway. Photograph 8-8 shows a stunning Flagstone Harlequin pattern.

Rare Patterns

Photograph 8-9   Rudy G. Weber
Ribbon or Flame Pattern
Not a harlequin because the angular pattern
does not fit closely together through the
entire opal.

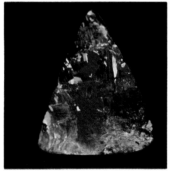

Photograph 8-10   Rudy G. Weber
Chinese Writing
in Boulder Opal

Photograph 8-11   Rudy G. Weber
Ribbon Pattern
Stone on left called
Harlequin by one dealer.

Rare Patterns

The above list does not come close to covering all the possible patterns. There are many rare or unusual patterns. Sometimes these patterns are called fancy patterns. Photographs 8-9 to 8-17 show examples of some of these patterns They give you an idea of the variety to be found in this wonderful stone.

Some rare patterns are repeated from time to time. For example, the *Mackerel Sky* pattern is quite rare but I have seen several examples (and own two of them). *Chinese Writing* is another rare pattern that is repeated often enough to have a generally accepted meaning.

There is no general acceptance of terms for most rare patterns. As an experiment I showed these pictures to various opal experts. The names they gave these patterns were quite varied. For example, the magnificent green-blue stone pictured in Photograph 8-9 has been described by various opal friends as a *Ribbon* pattern, a *Flame* pattern, and a *Flagstone Harlequin*. I would not agree to the last term because the stone does not meet the criteria of a regular angular pattern where all the patches of color fit together, although the left side is starting to look like a flagstone. The two stones in Photograph 8-11 are usually referred to as ribbon patterns, although they were called zebra pattern and the one in the upper left was called a harlequin by one person. The stone in Photograph 8-16 is

---

Naming rare patterns is fun, but differences among rare patterns have little effect on value.

---

sometimes called a *Zebra* pattern or a mackerel-sky pattern. The *Straw* pattern shown in Photograph 8-14, (also referred to by some of my opal friends as Chinese writing or an *Artist's Pallet*) is a thick variety of this pattern phenomena. If the bars of color overlap to look like a character in Chinese script, this would clearly be a Chinese writing pattern. (See Photograph 8-10.) Other stones which have been said to have a straw pattern are Photographs 8-12 and 8-13. The flame pattern shown in Photograph 8-15 derives its name,

More Rare Patterns

Photograph 8-12   Rudy G. Weber

Straw Pattern

Photograph 8-13   Len Cram

*Another interpretation
of Straw Pattern.*

More Rare Patterns

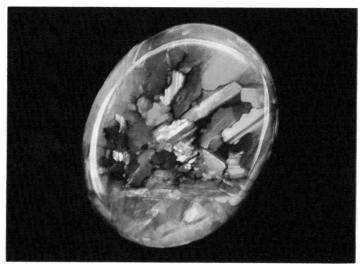

Photograph 8-14   Rudy G. Weber

*Yet another opal
called a Straw Pattern.*

Photograph 8-15   Rudy G. Weber

Flame Pattern

More Rare Patterns

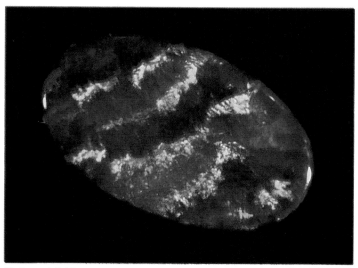

Photograph 8-16   Rudy G. Weber

Zebra or Mackerel Sky

Photograph 8-17   Len Cram

Ribbon or Mackerel Sky

as do most of the other rare patterns, from the fact that the pattern reminds one of a particular thing.

A great deal of time and effort could be spent acquiring pictures of rare patterns, describing each type, and giving it a name more or less consistent with general usage. Some hierarchy of value could then be established based on rarity and beauty. While such an exercise would be great fun, it would be of little practical use. Our goal is to define characteristics which determine value. Rare patterns are, well—rare. Thus they occur so infrequently that there is almost no information on how they affect market value. Such stones must be evaluated on a case-by-case basis. The rules of thumb which apply to other pattern classifications are not applicable in this case. Rare patterns are usually more valuable than flashfire patterns. That is about all that can be said. Since such patterns are rare, for practical purposes that is all that we really need to know.

Another type of rare pattern is a *chatoyant opal*. True chatoyancy is rare indeed. I have seen two types. One is a star formed in Idaho material. The star can be three-rayed or six-rayed. The same phenomena can produce a true cat's-eye opal. The first stones I saw that were claimed to be cat's-eyes were really rolling flashfire. But recently I have acquired a true cat's-eye. Another was reported by GIA.[21] These phenomena precious opals are rare indeed.

Picture Stones

The pattern in some stones paints a picture of something familiar. I call these *picture stones*. One example, illustrated in Photograph 8-18, is called the Glengarry Orchid because it was found in the Glengarry opal field near Lightning Ridge and reminds one of an orchid in full bloom. The Three Sisters (Photograph 8-19) reminds one of a rock formation of that name located in the Blue Mountains near Sydney. Sydney By Night (Photograph 8-20) reminds one of a night view of Sydney from a hill or high rise hotel. There are as many different names for picture stones as there are pictures captured in their fire patterns.

---

[21]"Cat's-eye Opal", *Gems & Gemology*, Fall, 1990, p. 232.

Photograph 8-18   *Rudy G. Weber*

The Glengarry Orchid

Named because the opal was found on the Glengarry Field and the pattern looks like an orchid.

Determining Pattern

To determine the pattern of a stone, compare it to the pictures in this Chapter. Most stones will have a flashfire pattern. When judging pattern, you must look for the dominant pattern in the stone. It is not uncommon to have more than one pattern present in a stone. You must choose the dominant pattern. As always, there will be some stones on the borders. Some judgment will be required. Be very careful not to use the term "Rare Pattern" too freely. Use

Picture Stones

Photograph 8-19   Rudy G. Weber

The Three Sisters

Named for the three spires in the Blue Mountains above Sydney that resemble the three red fire peaks in this boulder opal.

Photograph 8-20   Rudy G. Weber

Sydney By Night

Named for obvious reasons.

it only if the pattern is indeed rare *and* specially attractive. Also, be very careful with *harlequin*. I see perhaps one true harlequin per year. If a stone does not look like Photograph 8-6, 8-7 or 8-8, it is not correct to call it a harlequin.

There are as many wonderful patterns of fire as there are opals. However, the general categories presented here hold for any opal. Play the "Name That Pattern" game if you wish. It is great fun. But remember that the general broad categories I have presented here are all that is needed for valuing an opal.

Review

1. While every opal has a unique pattern, there are seven categories of patterns that all opals fit within: Pinfire, Flashfire, Broad Flashfire, Rolling Flashfire, Harlequin, Rare Patterns and Picture Stones.

2. Over 90% of all opals have patterns which fit into the flashfire or broad flashfire categories.

3. The term Harlequin is frequently misunderstood and mis-used. It refers *only* to regular square or angular patches of fire closely set together.

4. Rare Patterns are repeated periodically as opals are found. However the names used vary widely. It is more useful to refer to them under the general category of Rare Patterns.

5. Picture Stones remind one of something like a flower or a scene. The specific names are as varied as the pictures seem to show.

Chapter 9

Cut, Inclusions and Weight

Nobody's perfect. In diamonds, quality is judged by the 4 Cs: color, cut, clarity, and carat weight. So it is with opals. The preceding discussion concentrated on color (base color and fire color). In this chapter, we will turn our attention to the other 3 Cs. *Cut* refers to the way the opal has been shaped by the cutter. Inclusions (*clarity*) refer to imperfections in the stone which affect its beauty and wearability. *Carat weight* refers to the weight of the stone.

Cut

Opals are typically cut as cabochons. The shape or outline of the opal may be the familiar oval, but can include rounds, pears, marquise and freeform shapes. (See Figure 9-1.) Freeform shapes include all irregular outline stones, plus shapes such as squares and triangles. While I personally prefer freeform shapes, the market gives preference to ovals. Ovals can be cut to standard millimeter dimensions such as 6 x 4, 7 x 5, 8 x 6, or 10 x 8. When cut to standard size and shape they are referred to as *calibrated*. If oval, but not of standard dimensions, a stone is referred to as a *free size* or noncalibrated oval. Likewise rounds, pears, and marquise shapes may be calibrated or free size. The second element of shape is the degree of dome the stone has when viewed from the side. Degrees of dome include high-dome, medium-dome, low-dome, and flat.

While there is general agreement that high-domed stones are preferred, I find little evidence that medium- or low-domed stones are faulted in the marketplace. Especially when it is realized that some of the very best black opals from Lightning Ridge are cut as medium- or low-domed stones because the brilliant fire comes from a thin line of precious opal.

Figure 9-1

Types of Cut and Polished Opals

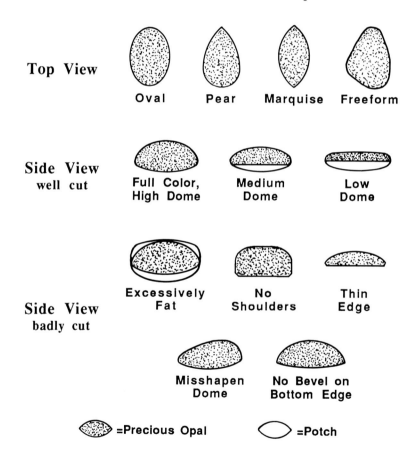

Top View			
Oval	Pear	Marquise	Freeform

Side View *well cut*

Full Color, High Dome	Medium Dome	Low Dome

Side View *badly cut*

Excessively Fat	No Shoulders	Thin Edge

Misshapen Dome	No Bevel on Bottom Edge

=Precious Opal   =Potch

Thickness is another element of shape. The usual problem is a stone which is cut so thin that it becomes fragile. A stone which is too thick is also a problem because it is unattractive. The ideal shape is a medium-high dome with a reasonable thickness and fairly thick shoulders on the stone. Such a stone along with some faulted shapes can be found in Figure 9-1.

Most opals on the market are well cut. Unfortunately, I see a fair number of poorly cut stones as well; and not stones cut by amateurs either. Even professional cutters in Hong Kong and Australia incorrectly cut opals on occasion. Sometimes this is done on purpose, such as the excessively fat stone in the lower right of Figure 9-1. This fat cut was done to make this stone heavier relative to the face or top view of the stone. Extra weight adds nothing to an opal's true value and, in fact, if carried to extremes, can reduce total price. Another common problem is a stone with no shoulder. Such a stone is almost impossible to set because prongs cannot securely hold the opal. Thin opals and opals cut with a thin edge are also a problem to set as they break very easily. Likewise, opals with a sharp edge will easily chip. There should be a bevel on the edge. Finally, the dome of a stone can be misshapen. Sometimes a stone is cut this way because of the shape of the rough. Even so, it is a less attractive shape and should be downgraded.

Thickness and Weight

How thick should a well cut opal be? There are no published guidelines, so I took some potch and cut stones of various shapes and sizes. I then judged the desirability of the shape. The result is the following general guide. (See Table 9-1.) Note that I have designated one shape and thickness as *ideal*. This is the most attractive shape in my judgment. The first listed shape is too thick. Such stones would look better if some of the back was cut off and/or shoulders cut. Also, the last listing is for stones I feel are too thin to look good and/or hold up in normal use.

> **Commercial calibrated ovals are usually thinner than ideal.**

TABLE 9-1
Weight and Thickness in Calibrated Oval Opals
Sizes*

Shape	18 x 13		16 x 12		12 x 10		10 x 8	
	Wt.	Thk.	Wt.	Thk.	Wt.	Thk.	Wt.	Thk.
Very Thick Flat Top (Too Fat)	11.86	8	8.25	6	4.12	5	3.27	5
Thick Flat Top	9.72	6	7.48	5	3.75	4.75	2.65	4
Nice High Dome (Ideal)	8.37	6	6.50	5	3.46	4.75	2.22	4
Medium Thick Flat Top	6.96	4	5.69	4	3.05	3	1.85	3
Medium Thick Regular Dome	5.99	4	5.15	4	2.53	3	1.47	3
Thin Flat Top	5.26	3	4.22	3	2.25	2	1.24	2
Thin Regular Dome (Too Thin)	4.98	3	3.76	3	2.06	2	1.10	2

*Note: Wt. = Weight in carats.   Thk. = Thickness in millimeters.

It is interesting to compare these shapes and weights to the calibrated oval cuts produced in Hong Kong. The average weight of sixty 10 x 8 ovals I have in my stock is 1.56 carats. They are typically 2.5 to 3mm thick. Thus, they are thinner (and flatter topped) than my ideal. This is because the cutters can obtain more weight of finished stones per ounce of rough opal if they cut medium thickness flat-topped stones. The extra yield can be 20% which implies at least a 10% increase in profit from the rough.

Thick cut stones and stones with a heavy rounded bottom are cut this way to increase their weight. Since opals are sold by the carat, a heavier stone increases price and profit. Many years ago cutters in Lightning Ridge started to cut black opals with a heavy bottom such as pictured on the center right in Figure 9-1. After a while buyers got wise to this extra weight and adjusted prices per carat accordingly. Still the tradition continues and even opals cut out of the seam material found in Glengarry and Sheepyard are cut with this rounded bottom. The rounded bottom of the stone in the lower left of Figure 9-1 is typical of white base and crystal stones cut by Hong Kong and other high-volume cutters. The added weight relative to a flat bottom may only be a few percent but summed over thousands of opals can increase profit. As in the case of black opals, prices have adjusted and such rounded bottoms are considered typical even though they make the opal harder to set safely. While I believe these rounded bottoms should have reduced values, they are now the norm in commercially cut opals, so normal prices build in this rounded bottom shape.

> # A high dome may be desirable,
> # but not necessary.

Some will argue that a flat-topped or low-domed stone is to be seriously faulted. I see little evidence of this in the market. The stone on the middle right of Figure 9-1 is a fairly flat-topped stone. Note that this stone would have been far less attractive if cut like the middle stone in the middle row. In fact, this flat-topped cut is fairly typical of the black opals found in Lightning Ridge because this cut shows the beauty of the stone to best advantage. While it is true that a high-domed stone such as the one at the middle left of Figure 9-1 is more valued, the difference is quite small in most cases.

Other elements of cut include polish and smoothness. A highly polished stone will have a high-gloss, glassy look to the surface when viewed with the unaided eye. Under a loupe some small scratches may be visible, and are acceptable if they cannot be seen without the loupe. A scratch that can be seen without the loupe should be faulted—the degree depending upon the affect on the beauty of the stone. The surface of the opal should be smooth.

> # Good cut includes a smooth,
> # high, polished dome.

Again, some sharp changes in shape or contour may be visible under a loupe but not without it. The opal should be faulted only if the lack of smoothness affects its beauty.

Here is a test to determine the smoothness of cut. Take the stone out of your grading light and look at the reflection of an overhead fluorescent bulb upon the surface of the stone. Pay no attention to color in this test. Focus only on the reflection. As you move the stone, a wavy cut will become obvious. This is a very demanding test and few stones pass it perfectly. You are only looking for serious irregularities.

It is important to distinguish waviness resulting from poor workmanship in cutting from the waviness that can result when a cutter is following an irregular line of color. It is sometimes necessary to almost carve the surface of the opal to expose the best color. This irregular carved surface is fairly common in boulder opals and in the clam shell opals found in Coober Pedy. Do not fault this waviness heavily unless it detracts from the beauty of the stone.

Many opals are polished on the back, many are not. To some, an unfinished back is a serious fault. To others, it makes no difference. I agree with this second group. I see no difference in the market between the value of an opal with a polished back and one that is neatly cut but not polished on the back. Only if the back is very irregular, has deep pits, or is highly scratched would it be found to be objectionable. Certain people claim that polishing the back of an opal will prevent it from crazing or cracking. I have not seen any difference between polished and unpolished backs in crazing.

All edges should be beveled.

All edges on opals should be rounded or beveled. A sharp edge is very likely to chip when the stone is set. Or, it may chip after some wear. In either case, sharp edges cause problems and should be considered faulty cutting.

Inclusions

All sources I know of agree that inclusions such as sand pits on the top of the opal that are visible to the unaided eye should be faulted. The degree of fault depends on the effect of the inclusion on the beauty of the stone. Inclusions of common opal, especially dark feathers, are also to be faulted but *only* if they affect beauty. Such imperfections are frequently ignored or given little weight in black opals unless they are so obvious and distracting that they ruin the look of the stone. Black lines can actually add to the attractiveness of a stone such as the Glengarry Orchid (Photograph 8-18) and would not be faulted.

Imperfections on the back of the stone are usually ignored. To quote one Australian source:

> "Marks in the face of an opal drastically affect value, although sand and inclusions on the base or inside which cannot be seen when looking at the top of the stone have little or no effect on value." (Their emphasis) Gemological Association of Australia, 1988.

Again the proviso should be added that this presumes the imperfections do not affect the *structural integrity* of the stone.

Cracks and Crazing

These are another matter. Cracks are severely faulted no matter where they appear in the stone. Like a crack in the window of a car, they tend to grow over time. Cracked stones eventually break. There are two types of cracks: One is a line or series of lines, usually curved, that look like stress fractures in glass. In fact, that is exactly what they are, stress fractures. The other type of crack is a closely knit and interlocking series of fractures that look like spider-webbing. This is called *crazing*. Photograph 9-1 is an example of a badly crazed opal.

Cracks are severely faulted.

To inspect an opal for cracks, hold the stone next to the edge of the shade on your lamp so that light passes through the stone to your eye. Cracks that come to the surface of the stone are visible as shadows and/or lines on the surface. Frequently they pierce through the fire pattern. Check the stone from all angles. Some surface cracks show only from particular angles. The internal part of these surface cracks will reflect orange light from one or more angles. You will be able to follow this orange reflection into the body of the stone. Internal cracks are more difficult to detect. Again, look at the stone from all angles, using transmitted light. Internal fractures will also reflect orange light. For some reason, many of these internal cracks are shaped like half-circles. Because they are internal, they often show the orange reflection from only one direction, so the stone must be examined carefully from all directions. At first, you may feel uncertain about recognizing cracks. After you have seen one or two, it will become quite easy to distinguish them.

Photograph 9-1   *Rudy G. Weber*

*Note the spider-web pattern
of cracks in this crazed opal.*

Distinguishing between cracks and natural structure lines can be tricky. Since a stone is downgraded in value very severely if cracked, great care must be taken not to condemn a good opal by confusing color lines for cracks. Many opal dealers in Australia and the United States have told me stories similar to the following: The dealer sells a stone to someone who then takes it to their local jeweler for an appraisal. The jeweler mistakes a color line or inclusion as a crack. The unhappy customer then demands their money back from the dealer. If what appears to be a crack does not show orange reflected light from at least one angle, it is not a crack but a structural change. Such changes are not faulted in an opal.

> # Don't confuse structural lines with cracks.

The three photographs reproduced here show two cracked stones (Photographs 9-1 and 9-2), and one that is not (Photograph 9-3). Note the shape of the fractures in the first two stones. Opal, having a structure like glass, breaks like glass. The curved nature of these cracks is typical of the conchoidal fractures found in opal.

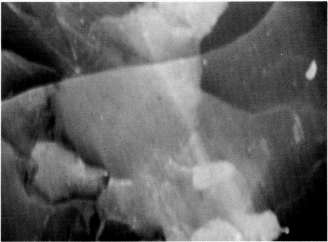

Photograph 9-2   *Rudy G. Weber*
Cracks cut across the fire pattern.

While the rounded shapes are common, some fractures are straight lines. Another telltale sign is when a fracture cuts across a pattern, as it does in Photograph 9-2. Structural changes do not cut across patterns. The beautiful black opal in Photograph 9-3 has two separate structures separated by a thin line of black potch. This structural separation is not a crack. Likewise, the flame pattern in the green-blue opal in Photograph 8-8 is not a crack. These lines are natural changes in the pattern of the opal.

Photograph 9-3   *Len Cram*
Line separating the two patterns is not a crack.

There is another phenomenon which is frequently misinterpreted as a crack. Refer to the lower left of the stone in Photograph 9-2. Note the irregular brown lines in the opal. These lines are brown potch separating sections of the opal, not cracks. The black opal in Photograph 9-3 has such inclusions, called feathers, in the dividing line between the two halves of the pattern. If these lines do not show the orange reflected light (See page 90), and they usually don't, they are not cracks. Frequently, black opals from Lightning Ridge will have these lines of potch separating the flashes of color.

Consistency and Directionality

Consistency refers to the sameness of brightness, color, pattern and density of the fire and the density and color of the background. Here I am going to ask you to make a judgment. An opal is never perfectly consistent in any characteristic. In talking about fire brightness, color, and pattern, I have told you to assess the dominant expression of the characteristic and ignore the rest. For example, brightness is judged by the overall impression the stone gives and the one little bright spot in a corner is ignored. Now what you must do, is look at each of these characteristics and note if it is consistent across the stone. If it is inconsistent, judgment is called for. Does the inconsistency add to or take away from the beauty of the opal? In most cases, a little inconsistency adds to the character of the stone and makes it more attractive. Such inconsistencies should not be faulted. Only when inconsistency causes an opal to be less attractive should it be faulted. For example, a large dark spot in the face of an otherwise light base color opal may distract from its beauty. If so, it should be faulted. But if the dark spot looks like a face, an animal, or a waterfall, it can give the stone character and maybe enhance its value. In Photograph 8-9 there is a change in the pattern over the upper right. This is an inconsistency, but in this case, it adds to the attractiveness of the opal. I am sorry I can't give you a visual criteria for when inconsistency becomes a problem. However, your judgment will serve you well.

Directionality of fire refers to whether the fire shows as brightly from one direction as it does from another.[22] Almost all opals will have some directionality in the brightness of fire. I say that some stones want to be rings (those that look brightest when looking straight down on them) and some want to be pendants (those that look brightest when held vertically and slightly behind the light).

> ## Some opals want to be rings and others want to be pendants.

---

[22]Miners commonly refer to this characteristic with the expression, "How the opal looks at you." A nondirectional stone "looks at you real well."

To assess directionality, hold the stone near the table 20" from the evaluation light. Now move the opal around and observe how the brightness of the stone changes. Hold the opal vertically and move it in the same way, observing differences in brightness. Rotate the stone. Most stones look best from one particular orientation. A truly nondirectional opal will appear equally bright no matter what direction you tilt it. Many stones will appear somewhat brighter in some directions than in others. An opal that looks bright from a direction which is not seen when it is worn is a less valuable stone. If the change is small, the stone would be graded *slightly directional*. If the change in brightness is at least one brightness level, the fire would be graded *somewhat directional*. If the stone looses most of its color from some directions, then it would be graded *very directional*. If it looses all of its fire in some directions, and especially if it only shows good color from one direction, it would be graded *highly directional*.

The more directional a stone the less valuable it is. Some stones show very bright color from the edge but are duller when viewed from the top. Pay no attention to the side color because it is not seen when the opal is worn. Broadflash patterns are frequently very directional. This is a problem for an opal used as jewelry because it does not show well except when the opal happens to hit this perfect orientation. However, if this opal can be oriented so that it usually shows the bright color when it is worn, the effect on value is less. Such a stone may look dull when laying on a table but if oriented correctly it can make a spectacular pendant.

Weight

This is fairly simple. Weight is in carats. Small stones of less than one carat are less valuable per carat and large stones of more than 40 carats are also lower in value. This value issue will be discussed further in Chapter 10.

While weight is fairly obvious in a loose opal, it is impossible to measure in a set stone. It is necessary to make an estimate. The data presented in Table 9-1 will help. Compare the length, width, and thickness of the stone to be estimated with the listings in the table. Interpreting between sizes will give you a fairly good idea of weight.

For freeform cut stones estimate the largest oval that could be produced from the stone if it were recut. Using length, width, and thickness, estimate the weight of this oval. The freeform stone will usually weigh from 1.5 to 2.0 times the oval. You must use your judgment of how much would be cut off in making the oval to come up with the appropriate multiple. The more you would have to cut off to make the stone an oval, the higher the weight multiple.

Boulder opals sell by the piece instead of by weight. The value of a boulder opal is determined by the size and quality of its opal face, not its weight.

In boulder opals, size is judged by the area of the opal face on the stone. They are classed as small, medium, large, and very large. Figure 9-2 gives the general size of boulder opals in the first three size categories. The very large boulder opals obviously are substantially larger than the large stones shown here.

There are a few dealers who sell boulder opals by weight. If you need to estimate the weight of a boulder opal, you have a difficult task. Ironstone is heavy. More importantly, the weight of a stone of a given size varies significantly with the density of the ironstone and the amount of it relative to the opal. This is why boulder opals are usually sold by the piece. Estimate the weight of

Figure 9-2

Sizes in Boulder Opal

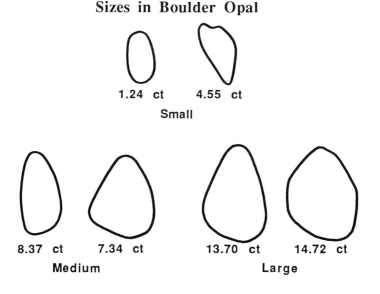

1.24 ct   4.55 ct
Small

8.37 ct   7.34 ct   13.70 ct   14.72 ct
Medium   Large

the stone as if it were all opal then add 10% to 20% depending upon the degree of ironstone found.

Cut, Inclusions, Cracks and Value

A well cut stone adds to the value of the opal. The stone should be well proportioned. A high dome is nice but not necessary. Excessively fat stones should be faulted if they make the opal less attractive. A poorly polished surface reduces the ability of light to enter and leave the opal, thus reducing brightness and value. Inclusions which are visible on the top of the stone and which detract from the beauty of the opal reduce value, but inclusions on the back usually do not affect value.

Cracked or crazed stones are seriously flawed. Opinions vary about their market value, but most opal dealers consider such stones valuable *only* as specimens. They are not considered to be of a quality to use in jewelry and thus have a very low value relative to a solid stone with the same characteristics.

Review

1.   Cut refers to the shaping of the opal. Most opals are cut into cabochons.

2.   The most popular shape of an opal cabochon is an oval. When ovals are of standard dimensions, they are referred to as calibrated opals.

3.   Poorly cut shapes include excessively fat stones, lack of a shoulder for setting, thin edges, misshapen dome, excessively thin stones, and the lack of a bevel on the bottom edge of the opal.

4.   Lightning Ridge stones are cut with a heavy belly to add weight to the stone. This belly has already been adjusted for in the opal's price per carat.

5.   Good cut also requires that the opal should be free from scratches visible to the naked eye and that it have a smooth surface. The exception is a boulder opal which may have a

carved irregular surface.

6. Inclusions which show on the face of an opal are faulted to the degree they reduce the visual appeal of the opal. Inclusions on the back or internal inclusions are ignored unless they reduce the structural integrity of the stone.

7. Cracks are detected by the orange light reflecting off their surface. If you do not see this orange light, the structure you are seeing is not a crack.

8. Distinguishing between cracks and natural structure lines is very important. An error here can condemn a good opal.

9. The very best stones are consistent as to pattern, fire color, background, etc. and are nondirectional. However, inconsistency and directionality are normal and should be seriously faulted only in extreme cases.

10. The weight of an oval can be estimated using Table 9-1. To estimate the weight of a freeform, estimate the weight of the largest oval that could be cut from the stone and multiply by 1.5 to 2.0.

A Celebration of Opals!

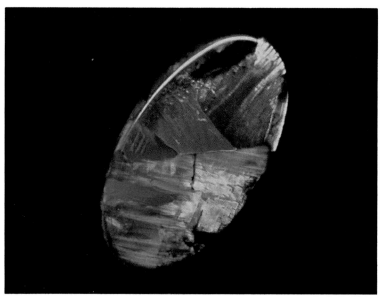

Rudy G. Weber

Len Cram

A Celebration of Opals!

Len Cram

Rudy G. Weber

A Celebration of Opals!

Len Cram

Rudy G. Weber

A Celebration of Opals!

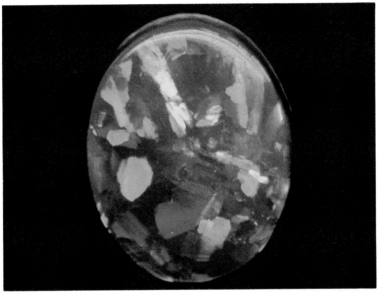

Rudy G. Weber

Rudy G. Weber

A Celebration of Opals!

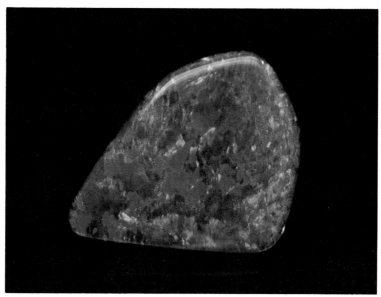

Len Cram

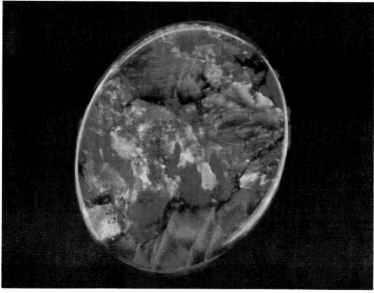

Rudy G. Weber

Chapter 10

Estimating the Value of Solid Cut Opal

The problem of valuing cut opals is considered to be the most difficult of all colored gemstone appraisals. The difficulties revolve around two primary problems—definitions and visual criteria. In the preceding chapters I have presented the definitions and visual criteria developed after years of experience with opals, and after long discussions with opal experts in Australia, Hong Kong, and the United States. With these definitions and criteria, you can now identify the most important characteristics that influence an opal's market value. The remaining problem is to place these characteristics into a value context. This is what I will do in this chapter. But first, I have to slip on my Economist hat to talk about what is meant by *value*.

Value

The concept of value is nebulous. Everybody seems to know personally what they mean by value but they are usually hard pressed to explain it to others. The opal you cut and set for your spouse has special meaning to both of you and, thus, a special value. This value transcends the money you paid for the rough opal and the gold. We might call this sentimental value. There is nothing wrong with this. It is common and desirable for you to acknowledge this highly personal special meaning, but the market will not give it weight.

The value sought when someone is asked to evaluate an opal is the price the opal would sell for in "the market." That is, the amount of money the opal would fetch in a transaction between two parties, a buyer and a seller. Some further specifications need to be added. The buyer and seller should be unrelated as to family or business. Thus buying an opal from your Aunt Sally does not count because she is likely to give you a lower price than the general market could sustain (or a higher one, you know Aunt Sally). A transaction between unrelated people may still not qualify if either buyer or seller is under special circumstances. A seller who is hard pressed for money may sell below market value. A buyer may be in special circumstances where they are more or less forced to buy. Such transactions are not true market transactions and do not give us a good idea of market value.

Market value, then, is the price resulting from a transaction between a willing buyer and an unrelated willing seller.

**Market value is set by a
willing buyer and a seller.**

We must now define which market we are referring to. There are many. Usually we think about wholesale and retail markets. But there are many different levels of wholesale markets and several different retail markets, each with somewhat different prices. Rather than discussing all possible prices, let's adopt a single *standard price*. The market price we will discuss is the price a retail customer would expect to pay at a quality retail jeweler. Such establishments are the backbone of the jewelry industry and reflect the vast majority of retail sales.[23]

---

[23]For wholesale prices, the following procedures are exactly the same. However, instead of using the data presented in Tables 10-2 to 10-6, look up the equivalent wholesale values in the latest issue of *The Guide*.

There are several other reasons why value estimates may differ widely. As noted in Chapter 1, no two stones are exactly alike. Preferences differ among people, and experience with opals differ widely as well. As a result, opinions of market value may differ significantly. The well defined and visual criteria we have presented will help reduce variations but it will not eliminate them. Opal valuation is still an *art*.

Valuing Solid Opals

The discussion in this chapter refers only to solid opals. Frankly, it is oriented to the solid opals from Australia since they represent the vast majority of all opals sold in the United States. These solid opals come primarily from four areas: Coober Pedy, Mintabie, Andamooka, and Lightning Ridge. There are solid opals found in areas of Queensland and White Cliffs, the main source of Australia's opals in the 1890s. They still produce a small volume. In addition, Brazilian opal fits into this category and would be valued identically to Australian solid opals. Solid opals from Mexico, Java, and the United States will be discussed in subsequent chapters.

The people of each mining area believe their opal is special and that it should sell at a premium. Understandable. However, once a stone is cut you can only guess at its origin. It is true that an experienced opal person can distinguish between fields for many stones but even they cannot tell in all cases. It is inevitable that once an opal is cut, it looses its origin. GIA says that cut stones should stand on their individual merit, not any claim of origin. For example, many of the Ceylon blue sapphires found in the market are from Australia, yet their origin is lost in international trade. Since origin is also very difficult to determine in cut opals, it should not be given extra weight in valuing a gem. I adopt GIA's stance with respect to the effect of origin on value in cut opals.[24]

Andamooka people argue that their stones do not craze and thus should be valued more highly. However, stones from White Cliffs, as well as most areas of Mintabie, Coober Pedy and Lighting

---

[24]In taking this stand, I probably have offended each of my friends in Australia. That is not my intention. I am just observing the facts as they are in the United States market.

Ridge do not craze either. Furthermore, once cut, the origin of an opal from any of these areas is lost. They all have more or less the same character. Some miners in Lightning Ridge believe that only The Ridge produces true black opals. Yet I have shown them Mintabie blacks (like my wife's ring), which they swear are from The Ridge. (See Photograph 10-1.) People argue that Brazilian opal should carry a premium because it is harder than Australian opal. But it is also more brittle and frequently indistinguishable from other cut opals. Thus, the market gives it no premium.

Photograph 10-1   Len Cram
The value of this ring is
independent of its origin.

When valuing an opal, it is safer to ignore any claims as to origin and not to take it into consideration in value. Having said this, I have included in the following chapters instructions on valuing opals from specific areas. This is not a violation of the rule above. These areas produce opals of a different type than the solid opals typical of the main sources in Australia. Because of these different characteristics, their evaluations require modifications to the general system found in the following methodology for solid opals.

Basic Step-by-Step Methodology

The following steps will allow you to develop a consistent estimate of the retail value of any solid cut opal. Follow each step carefully. It is tempting to skip a step. Don't do it. You may miss something that has significant affect on value.

Don't skip a step in the valuing process.

The procedure for valuing an opal can be broken down into two parts. The first part of the valuation process identifies the four primary determinants of an opal's value: type, base color, brightness, and weight. With these four characteristics you will be able to determine the price range for an opal. The second part of the valuation process uses the other characteristics which influence the value of an opal to narrow this price range to a specific value.

Part One:
Determining The Price Range

In order to determine the *Price Range* for the opal you are valuing, you must identify four major characteristics: Type, Base Color, Brightness of Fire, and Weight. To assist you in doing this consistently, an *Opal Evaluation Form* is presented on the following pages. Determine the *Type* of opal you are valuing using the information in Chapters 3 and 4. Enter that type in Part I of the form. Note that it is possible for the stone to have more than one type characteristic. For example, the opal could be a matrix opal and dyed.

Price range is determined by
- **Type**
- **Base Color**
- **Brightness of Fire**
- **Weight**

Determine the *Base Color* using the information and criteria presented in Chapter 5. Place an *X* next to the appropriate base color in Section II of the Opal Evaluation Form.

Determine the *Quality* from the relationship between the Brightness of Fire and Quality presented in Section III of the Opal Evaluation Form. Remember, to be accurate in assessing the brightness of the fire in your stone, you must compare it to the Opal

Opal Evaluation Form
Part One: Determining The Price Range

I. **Determine the Type of opal:**
Solid ____ Boulder ____ Matrix ____
Treated (Dyed) ____ Assembled ____
Synthetic ____ Simulant ____

II. **Determine Base Color**
Black ____ Semi-Black ____ Black Crystal ____
Crystal ____ Semi-Crystal ____ White or Gray ____
Orange ____ Other Color ____ Boulder Black ____
Boulder Brown ____ Boulder White ____

III. **Determine Quality from the relationship between brightness and quality listed below.** Circle the appropriate brightness.

Brightness of Fire	Quality
1	Less than Commercial
2	Commercial
3	Good
4	Fine
5	Extra Fine

IV. **Determine Weight or size of stone.**
Weight _____ carats
Size (Boulder opal only); Small ____ Medium ____
Large ____ Very Large ____

V. **Determine the Price Range for this opal:**
A. Select appropriate table given type and base color.
Enter Table number here_____ Line 1

B. Select appropriate cell in table given the quality and weight (size) of the opal.

C. Enter the **Price Range** present in this cell.
Price Range: _____ to _____ Line 2

Brightness Kit. As you will see shortly, an error here can throw your evaluation off by a large amount. Circle the appropriate brightness.

Determine the *Weight* of the opal. This is either a direct measurement or an estimate. (See Chapter 9.) Enter the weight in Section IV. Since boulder opals are sold by the piece instead of by weight, the size of the stone is judged by the size of its opal face as per Figure 9-2. Mark the stone size in Section IV.

The market value of an opal is primarily determined by the four characteristics discussed above. To obtain an estimate of market value, I use *The Guide*.[25] This source uses current market information gathered from a panel of dealers active in the United States opal market to estimate the wholesale prices for opals of various types and characteristics. In *The Guide*, a series of tables represent various types and base colors of opals. Each table further divides the opal into four qualities (the top four listed in Section III of the Opal Evaluation Form) and various weight (size) groups. Each entry in a table provides a range of price per carat (or per piece in the boulder opal case).

Tables 10-1 through 10-6 reproduce the tables found in *The Guide*. However, the price ranges reproduced here are not the wholesale prices. Instead they represent the retail prices you would expect to pay for these opals in a quality jewelry store. I have adjusted the price ranges to retail in consultation with *The Guide*.

To determine the price range for the opal you are valuing, select the appropriate table from Tables 10-1 through 10-6, using your assessment of opal type and base color as noted in Sections I and II. Enter the number of that table on Line 1. Next select the appropriate quality column from the relationship between brightness and quality in Section III of the Opal Evaluation Form. Then locate an appropriate weight (size) range under that quality. In that cell you will find a *Price Range* for the opal you are valuing. Enter this finding on Line 2 of Section V. If you are conducting a wholesale evaluation, take the values from the equivalent table in *The Guide*. Note that Tables 10-1 through 10-6 do not include matrix, dyed, assembled, synthetic, or opal simulants. These materials will be covered separately in subsequent chapters.

---

[25]*The Guide* is available from Gemworld International, Inc., 630 Dundee Road, Suite 235, Northbrook, IL 60062, (708) 564-0555.

TABLE 10-1

Black Opal: Retail Value in U.S. Dollars Per Carat.

Carat Weight	Commercial	Good	Fine	Extra Fine
1 to under 5	100 & up	300 - 1,400	1,400 - 8,000	8,000 - 20,000
5 to under 10	100 & up	300 - 1,400	1,400 - 8,000	8,000 - 20,000
10 to 15	100 & up	300 - 1,400	1,400 - 6,400	6,400 - 16,000

Source: Adjusted to Retail from *The Guide*, pp. 2-5, Oct. 1991.

NOTE: Extra fine black opals can be higher than the prices listed here, but opals of this quality are very rare and are almost never seen in the United States market

TABLE 10-2

Semi-Black & Crystal-Black Opal:
Retail Value in U.S. Dollars Per Carat.

Carat Weight	Commercial	Good	Fine	Extra Fine
1 to under 5	70 & up	300 - 1,200	1,200 - 3,000	3,000 - 5,000
5 to under 10	70 & up	300 - 1,200	1,200 - 4,000	4,000 - 7,000
10 to 15	70 & up	300 - 1,200	1,200 - 3,600	3,600 - 6,400

Source: Adjusted to Retail from *The Guide*, pp. 2-5, Oct. 1991.

TABLE 10-3

Crystal Opal: Retail Value in U.S. Dollars Per Carat.

Carat Weight	Commercial	Good	Fine	Extra Fine
1 to under 5	70 & up	150 - 500	500 - 1,000	1,000 - 2,000
5 to under 10	70 & up	150 - 500	500 - 1,000	1,000 - 2,400
10 to 15	70 & up	150 - 500	500 - 1,000	1,000 - 2,000

Source: Adjusted to Retail from *The Guide*, pp. 2-6 , Oct. 1991.

TABLE 10-4

Semi-Crystal Opal: Retail Value in U.S. Dollars Per Carat.

Carat Weight	Commercial	Good	Fine	Extra Fine
1 to under 5	30 & up	70 - 250	250 - 500	500 - 1,200
5 to under 10	30 & up	70 - 250	250 - 500	500 - 1,200
10 to 15	30 & up	70 - 250	250 - 500	500 - 1,200

Source: Adjusted to Retail from *The Guide*, pp. 2-6, Oct. 1991.

TABLE 10-5

White Base, Gray Base and Jelly Opal:
Retail Value in U.S. Dollars Per Carat.

Carat Weight	Commercial	Good	Fine	Extra Fine
1 to under 7	8 - 16	16 - 50	50 - 150	150 - 350
7 to under 15	16 - 50	50 - 100	100 - 220	220 - 350

Source: Adjusted to Retail from *The Guide*, pp. 2-7, Oct. 1991.

TABLE 10-6

Boulder Opal:
Retail Value in U.S. Dollars Per Piece.

Carat Weight	Commercial	Good	Fine	Extra Fine
Small (1-5 cts)	20 & up	100 - 1,800	1,800 to 5,000	5,000 to 10,000
Medium (5-10 cts)	20 & up	900 - 2,200	2,200 to 11,000	11,000 to 20,000
Large (10-15 cts)	20 & up	1,200 to 4,000	4,000 to 15,000	15,000 to 50,000
Very Large (over 15 cts)	20 & up	2,000 to 6,000	6,000 to 20,000	20,000 to 80,000

Source: Adjusted to Retail from *The Guide*, pp. 2-6, Oct. 1991

Part Two:
Determining A Specific Value

You have now produced an estimate of the price range of the opal you are valuing. Notice that this range is quite broad, probably unacceptably so. There are many different opals with substantially different characteristics which fit into any particular price range. Our goal in the second part of the opal valuing methodology is to use characteristics of a particular stone to narrow this range to an estimate of a specific price. (Opal Evaluation Form, Part Two.)

First we must determine the average price of opals in this Price Range. This can be done by adding the low and high prices in the range (Line 2) and dividing by two. This is the midpoint of the range. We will call this our *Base Price*. Enter the result on Line 3 in Section VI of the Opal Evaluation Form. All adjustments to price will be made from this Base Price.

Next we must determine the *Spread of Price*. This is calculated by subtracting the low price of the Price Range from the high price of that range (Line 2). Enter the result on Line 4, Section VI. We will use this Spread of Price to adjust the Base Price in subsequent steps.

We have learned in previous chapters that fire color, pattern, cut, shape, inclusions, cracks and crazing, consistency, directionality, and size influence the value of an opal. We will use these characteristics to narrow the Price Range to a specific price.

Table 10-7 presents value additions or subtractions for various characteristics of an opal. Each value in this table represents a percentage adjustment from the Base Price. The percentage adjustment is applied to the Spread of Price.

Note that there are two columns in this table—one for black and semi-black stones, and another for all other base colors. This is because black opal prices are more sensitive to the presence of certain characteristics than are other base colors.

This table tells us that an opal with blue only play of color will be -.50 times the Spread of Price less valuable than the Base Price, other things being equal.

In reading through Table 10-7, you can see that I have developed detailed descriptions of specific characteristics discussed in Chapters 7, 8, and 9. For each detailed description I have produced a specific value addition or subtraction. These values are based upon my experience in the opal market and extensive discussion with other opal experts. The reasoning behind these values will be presented in a subsequent section of this chapter. To determine the value additions or subtractions for the opal you are valuing, list all the relevant characteristics in the *Findings* column in Section VII of the Opal Evaluation Form. Look up each characteristic in the appropriate column of Table 10-7 and enter the numeric value on the appropriate line of the *Value Additions* column. For example, if the opal you are valuing has only blue fire note "blue only" under Findings, and enter "-.50" under Value Additions. For some characteristics you are given a range of values. In such cases I am asking you to exercise some judgment. Does a poor cut reduce the attractiveness of the stone a little or a lot? If a little, enter "-.10" under Value Additions. If a lot, enter "-.50".

Use These Characteristics

- **Fire Color**   • **Pattern**
- **Dome**   • **Cut**
- **Shape**   • **Inclusions**
- **Cracks**   • **Consistency**
- **Directionality** • **Size**

To Narrow Price Range to A Specific Price.

Once you have examined each characteristic listed in Section VII and entered the appropriate addition (subtraction), enter the sum on Line 5, *Total Value Additions* in Section VII. Note that this value may be positive or negative and can be larger than one (1).

Total Value Addition is used to adjust the Base Price for the opal you are valuing. The *Base Price Adjustment* is calculated by multiplying the Spread of Price (Line 4) by the Total Value Addition (Line 5). Again, the value you enter in Line 6 of Section VIII can be positive or negative.

Opal Evaluation Form
Part Two: Determining A Specific Value

VI.   **Determine Base Price and Spread:**

    A.   **Base Price** - Calculate the midpoint of the Price Range (Line 2) and enter here:
Base Price: _____   Line 3

    B.   **Spread of Price** - Calculate the spread by subtracting the low price in the Price Range from the high price.
Spread of Price: _____   Line 4

VII. **Determine Value Additions (Subtractions) to Base Price:**

    A.   Enter the relevant characteristics for this opal in Finding column below.

    B.   Enter value additions (subtractions) from Table 10-7 in Value Addition column below.

Characteristics	Finding	Value Addition
Fire Color	_____	_____
Pattern	_____	_____
Dome	_____	_____
Cut	_____	_____
Shape	_____	_____
Inclusions	_____	_____
Cracks	_____	_____
Consistency	_____	_____
Directionality	_____	_____
Size	_____	_____

    C.   Total value additions (subtractions) and enter here:
Total Value Addition (subtraction) _____Line 5

VIII. **Determine Base Price Adjustment:**
Calculate Base Price Adjustment by multiplying the Spread of Price (Line 4) by Total Value Addition (subtraction) (Line 5): Base Price Adjustment =

$$\underset{\text{Line 4}}{\underline{\qquad\qquad}} \; x \; \underset{\text{Line 5}}{\underline{\qquad\qquad}} \; = \; \underline{\qquad\qquad}\text{Line 6}$$

IX.   Determine **Adjusted Base Price:**
Calculate Adjusted Base Price by adding (subtracting)
Base Price (Line 3) and Base Price Adjustment (Line 6)
and enter below:

Adjusted Base Price Per Carat (piece) =

$$\underset{\text{Line 3}}{\underline{}} + \underset{\text{Line 6}}{\underline{}} = \underline{} \qquad \text{Line 7}$$

X.   Determine **Total Estimated Price:**
Calculate Total Estimate Price by multiplying Adjusted
Base Price per carat (Line 7) by weight of opal in
carats. (Step not needed for Boulder Opals.)

Total Estimated Price:

$$\underset{\text{Line 7}}{\underline{}} \times \underset{\text{Weight}}{\underline{}} = \underline{} \qquad \text{Line 8}$$

XI.   **Final Review and Adjustment:**
Adjust price *and* give reasons below *if*
Total Estimated Price is inappropriate.

The *Adjusted Base Price* is calculated by adding (subtracting) the Base Price Adjustment (Line 6) to the Base Price (Line 3). Enter the resulting Adjusted Base Price on Line 7 of Section IX. You have now calculated a specific price per carat (or per piece for boulder opals) for the opal you are valuing.

To determine the *Total Estimated Price* of the opal you are valuing, simply multiply the Adjusted Base Price (Line 7) by the opal's weight. Enter this total on Line 8 in Section X. Skip this step for boulder opals since they are priced per piece rather than per carat.

You have now completed an evaluation of the market price of this opal. But there is one last step and it requires some judgment. The methodology I have presented is rather straight forward and mechanical even though it is unavoidably complex. However, an opal, like a sports team, can be more or less than the sum of its parts. As a final step, look at the opal again and gain an overall

TABLE 10-7

Characteristics & Description	Value Addition or Subtraction	
	All Other Stones	Black, Semi-Black Black Crystal
Fire Color:		
Blue only	-.50	-.50
Green only	-.10	-.20
Blue-Green	-.05	-.10
Green-Blue	.00	-.10
Green-Orange	.00	+.10
Orange-Green	+.05	+.15
Red only	+.05	+.25
Orange-Red	+.10	+.30
Multicolor	+.10	+.30
Red multicolor	+.20	+.40
Red-Blue multicolor	+.25	+.50
Pattern:		
Pinfire	-.05	-.05
Flashfire	.00	.00
Broad Flashfire	.00	.00
Rolling Flashfire	+.10	+.10
Harlequin	+.20	+.20
Rare Patterns and Picture Stones	+.00 to +.20	+.00 to +.20
Dome:		
Low-dome	-.10	-.10
Medium-dome	.00	.00
High-dome	+.10	+.20
Cut:		
Poor cut or finish	-.10 to -.50	-.10 to -.50
Excessively fat cut	-.10 to -.50	-.10 to -.50
Shape:		
Standard Oval	+.15	.00
Other standard shapes	.00	-.20
Free size Oval	.00	.00
Freeform Shapes	-.20	-.30
Carvings	+.10 to -.30	+.10 to -.30
Inclusions:		
Badly included	-.20 to -.50	-.20 to -.50
Slightly included	-.15	-.15
Not included	.00	.00
Cracked (Crazed):		
Cracked (Crazed)	**No value as jewelry**	**No value as jewelry**

Consistency of Brightness and Pattern:			
	Major dull spot	-.20	-.20
	Minor dull spot	-.10	-.10
	Undesirable pattern mix	-.20	-.20
	Distracting variation in base color or density	-.20	-.20
	Consistent	.00	.00
Directionality:			
	Highly directional	-.30	-.30
	Very directional	-.20	-.20
	Somewhat directional	-.05	-.05
	Slightly directional	.00	.00
	Not directional	+.10	+.10
Size:	.50 carat to .99 carat	-.20	-.30
	.00 carat to .49 carat	-.30	-.50
	15 carats to 20 carats	-.15	-.15
	20 carats to 30 carats	-.20	-.20
	30 carats to 40 carats	-.25	-.25
	Above 40 carats	-.30	-.30

impression of its beauty. Ask yourself if the value in Section X seems to fit the opal. If it seems high or low, try to figure out why. Sometimes this review will convince you that an inclusion is more (or less) detrimental than you thought, or some other characteristic should be reevaluated. Then you can adjust the appropriate entry on the Opal Evaluation Form, and recompute Line 8. In another case you may not be able to identify exactly why, but you feel the price on Line 8 is not quite correct. Feel free to adjust the value somewhat. The process should not be too mechanical. But if you do adjust the Total Estimated Price, write down the adjustment and your reasoning in Section XI of the Opal Evaluation Form.

An Example

In order to make sure that I have explained the process completely, let me give you an example of how it would work. Suppose you wished to value the following stone. The opal to be valued is a standard 10 x 8 oval in a semi-crystal base. It has a flashfire pattern of orange-green fire. The brightness of this fire is Level 3. It is well cut, with a medium dome and no inclusions or cracks. The pattern is quite consistent. The fire, however, is

Table 10-8
Example Of An Opal Valuation

Part One:

I.   Type is <u>Solid</u>.

II.   Base Color is <u>Semi-crystal</u>.

III.   Quality is <u>Good</u> (Brightness Level 3).

IV.   Weight is <u>1.50</u> carats

V.   A. The appropriate table is <u>10-4</u>, Line 1.

        B. The price range is <u>70</u> to <u>250</u>, Line 2.

Part Two

VI.   A. Base Price is (70 + 250) ÷ 2 = <u>160</u>, Line 3.

        B. Spread of Price is 250 to 70 = <u>180</u>, Line 4.

VII.   A & B:

Characteristic	Finding	Value Addition
Fire Color	Orange-Green	+.05
Pattern	Flashfire	.00
Dome	Medium-Dome	.00
Cut	Good	.00
Shape	Standard Oval	+.15
Inclusions	None	.00
Cracks	None	.00
Consistency	Consistent	.00
Directionality	Somewhat	-.05
Size	1.5 carats	.00

        C. Total Value Addition   <u>+.15</u>, Line 5

VIII.   Base Price Adjustment: <u>180</u> x <u>+.15</u> = $27.00, Line 6
                               Line 4   Line 5

IX.   Adjusted Base Price: <u>160</u> + <u>27.00</u> = $187.00, Line 7
                             Line 3   Line 6

X.   Total Estimated Price <u>187.00</u> x <u>1.50</u> = $280.50, Line 8
                              Line 7   Weight

XI.   A review of the overall stone leads me to conclude that the price on Line 8 is about right.

directional. The opal weighs 1.50 carats. With these characteristics defined, we can now value the opal. The results are shown in Table 10-8.

Reasons for Weightings

Steps I through V provide a range of price for any solid or boulder opal based upon the four primary characteristics—type, base color, brightness and size. Steps VI through XI modify that range of price to produce a specific value based upon the other characteristics discussed in Chapters 7 through 9.[26] The adjustments for various characteristics represent my interpretation of how these affect market value (after consultation with other opal experts, of course). Note that there are different values for some characteristics in the Black, Semi-Black and Black Crystal column. This is because the market for these stones differs somewhat from the White and Crystal base stones.

I know this is a long list of characteristics and weightings. However, it represents the fine tuning necessary if your value estimate is to be a fair representation of the current market value of the opal in question. A discussion of the reasoning behind the weights presented in Table 10-7 will help to set them in your mind.

Fire Color: In general the more red or orange fire colors present, the higher the market value. This is because these colors are found to be more attractive by most people. In black opals any orange or red significantly enhances value. Blue-green and green-blue fire had been less valued in the United States, but recently these combinations have been gaining more favor here. These colors are highly prized in the Orient. Consequently the prices of blue-greens and green-blues are now not much less than orange-greens. Make sure that a blue only stone shows a pattern of color, not just an iridescent blue sheen. If the opal only has an opalescent sheen, it is not a precious opal and is valued even less. Such stones are called jelly opal. When cut as cabochons, jelly opal has little value.

---

[26]While the methodology presented here is discussed in terms of *The Guide*, any other source of opal value may be used. The basic parameters here still apply.

However, when faceted it can be quite attractive and fits into the value structure in Table 10-5.

Pattern: Generally speaking a larger pattern (bigger chunks of fire) is more showy and thus more valuable. Rare patterns increase an opal's value *only* if they make it more attractive. The more interesting and beautiful the pattern, the more it affects value. True harlequins are rare indeed. Be very careful to reserve this term only for opals which meet the visual criteria presented in Chapter 8.

Cut: Generally a high dome makes the opal more attractive and thus more valuable. Flattish tops are less preferred but do not have as much effect on value as some writers have stated. This is especially true with black opals where fairly flat stones are common. Excessively fat stones should be adjusted to reflect both the increase in weight that results *and* the reduction in attractiveness. Visible scratches and flat spots will reduce value, the degree depending upon how the fault affects the beauty of the stone.

Shape: In white and crystal stones the oval is the generally preferred shape. If the oval is of a standard shape it fits into volume produced standard mountings easily. This makes setting less expensive. The savings in mounting costs is partly reflected in an increase in price for calibrated ovals.[27] Freeform shapes are harder to set so they sell at a discount. It is interesting to note that once set, freeform stones may sell for as much or more than ovals. Many people find them more attractive. In black opals the acceptable shape is oval. Since these stones are so valuable, they are seldom cut into calibrated size. Thus custom mounting is the norm and no premium is paid for standard sizes. Any shape other than oval is penalized because the Japanese market rejects them, or at least it has in the past. You will rarely see a black that is not an oval unless it is a highly unusual pattern which would be ruined by cutting an oval. The other exception is cases where someone like myself has cut the opal and designed the setting, rather than offering the black opal unset on the market. I refuse to waste beautiful opal by forcing it into an oval shape.

Inclusions and Cracks: The borderline between degrees of problems with inclusions is very imprecise. As explained in Chapter 9, some judgment is required on the effect of an inclusion on the

---

[27]Unfortunately, standard settings are seldom set up to protect opals from cracking when worn. This is a fault of the setting, not the opal.

beauty and thus the value of the opal. While I have presented a range of -.20 to -.50 in Table 10-7 for badly included stones, there could be cases where inclusions reduce the value for jewelry purposes to zero. Cracked or crazed stones are not valuable as jewelry and opal experts do not feel they would have any market value except as specimens. For example, one Australian publication states, "The basis for valuation of minor crazing in an opal of 25% of its normal *clean* price is fair; while a low 10% of its normal price for heavily crazed stones is more conservative.[28]" The author goes on to note that retailers in Australia and the United States differ with this low value "particularly if he owns one." I have discussed this matter with many jewelers and salespersons in stores over the United States and generally the opinion they express is that all opal is or will be crazed and crazing doesn't affect value. *However, when these same jewelers are buying opals they will not buy any crazed or cracked stones, no matter what the price. Obviously, crazing does drastically reduce value.*

Cracked opal is not valuable for jewelry.

Consistency: Most opals are fairly consistent in brightness and pattern. If a cutter finds inconsistent rough he or she will cut smaller, relatively consistent stones from it. Thus serious consistency problems are rare in professionally cut stones. But they do occur so you still have to check for them.

Directionality: Directionality cannot be easily avoided in cutting, so you will see more highly directional stones on the market. Directionality is a particular problem with broadflash patterns. Again, judgment is needed. Keep in mind that directionality is a problem only to the extent it affects the beauty of the opal when it is worn.

Size: Bigger is preferred to smaller as you can see from Tables 10-2 to 10-6. However, once a stone becomes very large it's value as jewelry starts to decline. This is because it is too big to be

---

[28]M. Duncan, "Crazing of Stones," *Gemline* (publication of the Australian Gem Industry Association), October, 1988.

worn comfortably. Usually such big stones (over 40 carats) are cut into smaller stones to avoid this problem. Stones of less than a carat, usually small calibrated stones like 6 x 4, 7 x 5 or 8 x 6 ovals, sell at a lower price because they are less attractive and the rough to cut them is more readily available. Preferred ring sizes are 10 x 8 to 12 x 10 (1½ to 4 carats). Pendants generally are larger, but seldom bigger than 18 x 13 (8 to 10 carats). Partly it is the nature of the rough that causes this smaller size, as large chunks of rough are more difficult to find.

The value of large stones above 15 carats is not included in *The Guide*. Such large stones are found in the market, so we need a relationship between weight and value. Such a relationship is presented in Table 10-7. Care must be exercised in using these or any other weightings. A large stone that is large because of pattern or especially high quality would not be reduced in value as much as indicated in the table.

Overall Beauty of an Opal

The last step is to look at the opal and get a final overall impression of the stone. The methodology presented here is intended to be a guide to value, not the final word. After all, it is the overall beauty of the opal that is the clincher. All these details, while important, do not tell the full story. Does the evaluation price seem reasonable? If you feel it is a bit too high or too low, adjust accordingly. Usually no adjustment will be necessary, but occasionally the stone is more (or less) than the sum of its parts. It is unfair to the stone not to take this into consideration. But adjust for a reason, and be sure you know why you are making the adjustment.

Guarantee

The Guide states that opal prices are for guaranteed stones. However, there is no statement about what is guaranteed. Indeed, there is no industry standard on guarantees.

First we have to determine what is guaranteed. Two things can happen to an opal—cracking and crazing. Cracking results from pressure or force applied to the opal from outside. A prong tightened too much or a whack on the stone from the wrong angle can crack an opal just as it can crack a diamond. Crazing results from the deterioration of the internal structure of the opal. Some feel it results when the opal drys out. Others feel that it is the result of chemical restructuring.

Whatever the cause, opal dealers typically will guarantee cut opals against crazing for some period of time. They typically will not guarantee the stone against cracking. This is because cracking comes from mistreatment by the purchaser while crazing results from internal flaws in a stone.

How can the two be distinguished? In most cases the difference is fairly obvious. Crazing starts at the surface of the opal proceeding around the stone but not into it until well into the process. The breaks are very fine and often interlocking as Photographs 9-1 and 9-2 show. Cracks resulting from force start at an edge and usually go deep into or through the opal. They are straight or conchoidal. There is usually only one crack.

The opal dealer will reserve the right to make the determination of whether the opal has crazed or been cracked.

The length of time for a crazing guarantee can be as little as zero or as long as the life of the owner. Although there is no industry standard, a one-year guarantee is the most common. This is the verbal guarantee given most often by Lightning Ridge miners.

If an opal crazes under a guarantee, the usual remedy is for the dealer to replace the stone with another of equal quality. They can never guarantee to replace the stone with one of identical characteristics as they could search for years and not find one. Again, the dealer reserves the right to be final arbitrator on "equivalent quality." In a few cases the guarantee may offer a refund instead, but I have never seen such a guarantee in writing.

Guarantees are legal statements. They must be in writing to have any real chance of being enforceable.

Fossils

Opal replacement of clam shells can produce some very attractive specimens. Most of the clam shell opals found on the market are from Coober Pedy. They are white, semi-crystal, and occasionally crystal. Many are cut into cabochons, thus losing their unique fossil characteristics. Some are polished to retain their original clam shell shape. They can make unique and popular pieces. Polished clam shells are valued like other cut stones except a downward adjustment must be made for the extra thickness and difficulty in setting these stones. About 10 to 30% is correct, depending upon how much of the clam shell shape has been retained. Be especially careful to look for sand inclusions which may compromise the structural integrity of the finished piece.

Other fossils are found throughout the Australian fields. In the past most were cut into cabochons and their fossil origin destroyed. Nowadays some are preserved. These are valued as fossils and as opal. The main fossil other than clam shells that shows up as polished opal is a belemnite. Again this is found in Coober Pedy. It is a long round prehistoric squid-like creature replaced by opal. Care must be taken in valuing these fossils. They have additional value (about 10%) *only* when the polished piece retains enough of the original fossil's shape to be readily recognized. Fossil shapes can be faked by a cutter, although this is uncommon.

Fossils of plesiosaurus, a reptile, have been found in several locations. Some claim to have uncovered tiger teeth. Parts of other animals have been opalized. These rare fossils are not common enough to have a clear market value.

Pineapples are a strange formation found only in White Cliffs. They are really a replacement of a crystal formation that looks like a pineapple. The crystal they are replacing is a subject of great controversy which has yet to be fully settled. They are quite unique and are not cut up or polished. They sell by the piece (when available which is rarely). The prices range from $5,000 up, depending on the shape of the pineapple and the amount of fire it contains.

Conclusion

The methodology presented here will allow you to estimate the value of any solid opal in the crystal, white, gray, and black base color range. Because of the visual guides provided in previous chapters, your evaluation should not differ materially from mine, or anyone else who uses this system. If your evaluation does differ significantly from someone else, a comparison of Opal Evaluation Forms will expose the differences. A discussion of the characteristics and their weighting should easily resolve differences. This consistent evaluation based on visual, measurable and reproducible criteria is my goal.

Remember that the methodology is intended only as a guideline. Any mechanical system cannot hope to take into consideration all the subtleties that each opal offers. You must use your judgment when you get to the bottom line. Also remember that the opal market is active and, therefore, constantly in flux. That is why I use as a base for the pricing a publication which is periodically revised to reflect changes in the market. Conditions do not change overnight, but they do change, so you must consult an up-to-date source for base prices.

Review

1. Market value is the price resulting from a transaction between a willing buyer and a willing seller.

2. Because origin cannot be accurately determined when a solid opal has been cut, the market assigns it no role in the value of cut solid opal.

3. An estimate of the value of an opal can be obtained using the step-by-step methodology presented in the Opal Evaluation Form.

4. Retail prices can be obtained by employing Tables 10-1 through 10-6. To obtain wholesale prices, consult the relevant tables in *The Guide* or any other source of wholesale value you find acceptable.

5. The values in Tables 10-1 through 10-6 and the weightings in Table 10-7 represent current market conditions as of 1992. As market conditions change, prices and weights may have to be adjusted.

Rudy G. Weber

*Beauty like this is the reason why
boulder opals are increasing rapidly in price.*

Chapter 11

Estimating Boulder Opal Value

The best boulder opals may rival black opals in beauty (notice that I did not say they surpass them). The photographs in this Chapter give evidence of this beauty. In fact, some people prefer boulder opals to any other type.

Boulder opal has been gaining rapidly in popularity throughout the world over the last few years. Ten years ago it was well behind crystal and semi-black solid opal and, of course, far below black opals in popularity. Now it is second only to black opal in preference. In value it is quite nearly equal to semi-black and black crystal and ahead of crystal. And why not? Boulder opals are strong, unique, and offer a range of patterns and a character different from any other opal.

Their rapid rise to fame has come without much knowledge of this type of opal in the retail trade. So before I turn to discussions of value, let me give you a bit of history.

A Brief History of Boulder Opal

The first Australian opal to hit the world market in the late 1800s was from Queensland. Originally I assumed that this opal was the boulder opal we are now familiar with. In fact, it was not. The first opal from Queensland was pure red multicolor crystal. It was found in pipes and in seams in the brown ironstone that is the base for boulder opal. Back then, only seams thick enough to cut solid opals were valued. The thin seams that make up the faces of most boulder opals today were considered too thin to be useful and were discarded or used in trade with the local ladies for their "favors." Hence the name "fun stones." Most of the finished stones were small. It was not until the discovery of White Cliffs in 1884 that seam opal, which cuts much larger stones, entered the market.

Incredible as it seems now, the beautiful thin seams of red multicolor boulder black opal that can now sell for $5,000 to $250,000 per piece, were thrown away back then. It was not until the late 1950s and into the 1960s that boulder opal made any impression in the world market. It was then that Des Burton, Joy Clayton, and John Traurig, among others, made a concerted effort to introduce it to the world. Its popularity grew, but not until the 1980s did it explode. With this newly found popularity came rapid increases in prices. It is not uncommon for jewelers who have not purchased boulder opal for a couple of years to suffer from "sticker shock" when told the prices that boulder opal now commands.

It is difficult to get the value of boulder opal right. Because of its explosion in value, prices have not settled down. It is almost as if the old adage that "an opal is worth whatever someone will pay for it" has come true in spades. Add to the rapid explosion of prices the fact that some dealers price boulder opal by the piece, while others price it by the carat, and it can be seen that we have a difficult task in front of us. Keep in mind as you read and use this discussion of boulder opal prices that all opinions are subject to change in this highly volatile market.

Types of Boulder Opal

Boulder opal is divided into two main types—seam boulder opal and boulder matrix opal.

Boulder Opal : The seam type, referred to just as a boulder opal, consists of seams of opal of varying thickness formed in a dense brown ironstone such as Photograph 3-3 and Photograph 11-1. The seams are often irregular. To produce a stone, the cutter must follow these irregular thin seams. The result is an opal with an irregular surface. While smooth surfaced boulder opals are preferred, these irregular surfaced stones are now common in the market.

Photograph 11-1   *Len Cram*
Boulder opal showing a thin seam of opal on ironstone.

Split Faces. Since the opal is more prone to fracture than the ironstone in which it is found, sometimes boulder opal seams are split to expose a matched pair of opals. Such boulder opals are called split faces. The process can be explained with the use of Photographs 11-2A and 11-2B. First the ironstone is ground down until the seam is exposed all around its edge. Next, a blunt screwdriver is placed

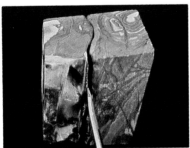

Photograph 11-2A   *Rudy G. Weber*   *Photograph 11-2B*   *Rudy G. Weber*

on the seam of opal as in Photograph 11-2A. Then you hold your breath and give the end of the screwdriver a good whack with a hammer. If you are lucky, the seam splits to expose two faces as in Photograph 11-2B.

Split face boulder opals are usually not polished. Instead the fractured surfaces are left natural since they have as good a polish as can be put on by a cutter. All that needs to be done to complete the stones in Photograph 11-2B is to shape them and round the edges slightly. Split faces are not real common and usually command a premium price.

Photograph 11-3   *Len Cram*

Boulder Matrix: Boulder matrix is a combination of opal and ironstone where the opal is all mixed through the ironstone rather than in seams. Photographs 3-4 and 11-3 are examples of the two main types of boulder matrix opal. Photograph 3-4 is matrix from a small area in southwestern Queensland called Yowah. It is highly prized for the unusual patterns of opal found in the matrix. Photograph 11-3 is an example of Mainside boulder matrix (usually referred to as just Mainside Matrix) found farther up in western Queensland near Jundah. Many other areas throughout western Queensland produce similar boulder matrix. Boulder matrix is usually cut with a smooth surface. Ovals and freeforms are cut from the Mainside Matrix while the Yowah material is almost always cut into freeforms.

While both seam and matrix types follow many of the same rules in valuing, there are some differences. Consequently, I will first discuss the seam type, referred to as just boulder opal, and hold the discussion of boulder matrix until later in the chapter.

Valuing Boulder Opal

This is a most frustrating section of the book to write. On the one hand, boulder opal should, and does, submit to the same methodology as other opal when determining value. On the other hand, there is more variability in people's opinions on boulder opal value than on other types of opal.

While some dealers are now selling boulder opal by the carat, *The Guide* offers per piece prices for boulder opal so we will stick with this time-honored approach. There are several adjustments necessary to make the system presented in Chapter 10 work for boulder opal.

Following the Opal Evaluation Form, the first entry is type. Here there is no problem as all are one type—boulder opal. Next is base color. In fact, boulder opal can come with black, semi-black, white, orange or crystal on brown, and jelly on brown base colors. Herein lies our first problem.   The boulder opal table presented in

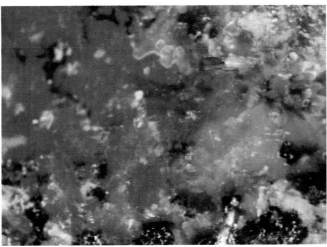

Photograph 11-4   *Rudy G. Weber*
Magnificent Boulder Black Opal

The Guide and reproduced in retail version in Table 10-6, works well for boulder opals that face black. For other base colors, major adjustment must be made.

Boulder Black: Boulder black opals have a rich fire color on a dark black background. An excellent example is in Photograph 11-4. If you look at the edge of a boulder black, you can often see a very thin line of black potch between the opal and the ironstone. Such boulder blacks are the cream of the boulder opals and the ones that command the premium prices listed in Table 10-6. In fact, one rule of thumb I have heard is that boulder blacks are about one-third the price of equivalent Lightning Ridge blacks.

To value a boulder black analyze its characteristics just as you would a solid opal. Use the additions and subtractions of regular opal in Table 10-7. However, when you get to cut, inclusions, and cracks (Section VII), two special adjustments must be made. The prices in Table 10-6 are for smooth faced boulder blacks without *any* ironstone inclusions in the face. The first adjustment is for an irregular carved opal surface. An irregular surface is valued 10% to 30% less than a smooth faced boulder opal, depending upon the degree of irregularity of the surface and its effect on the beauty of the stone. If a boulder opal has a carved face, enter -.10 to -.30 in the Value Addition column, Section VII, under dome.

> ## Irregular surfaced boulder opals
> ## are less valuable.

The second adjustment is for the degree of ironstone inclusions in the face of the opal. Table 10-6 presumes there are none. In Table 11-1, discounts are presented for various degrees of ironstone inclusions. Note that just a small ironstone inclusion reduces the value 30% of the range in price. Actually one dealer suggested that a small inclusion reduced the value by 50% or more. I believe that is a bit high. Obviously, a very seriously included stone has a large discount applied to it.

Photographs 11-5 through 11-8 show boulder opals with various degrees of precious opal in their faces. Clean, smooth faced

Photograph 11-5   Rudy G. Weber

Clean faced boulder opal

Photograph 11-6   Rudy G. Weber

*There is a small degree of ironstone
in the face of the lower stone.*

Photograph 11-7   *Rudy G. Weber*
More ironstone inclusions in the face

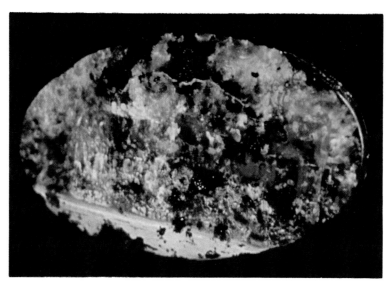

Photograph 11-8   *Rudy G. Weber*
Ironstone inclusions and common orange potch

boulder opals, such as those in Photograph 11-5, are the most preferred. Note that when inclusions reach a large percentage of the face, as they do in the lower stone in Photograph 11-7, they become quite distracting. In Photograph 11-8, another phenomena is present, potch opal. When potch or jelly opal is present in the face of a boulder opal, the potch or jelly is counted as an inclusion, just as the ironstone is counted. Thus the orange potch in the right of this stone would count as an inclusion and reduces the percentage of precious opal in the face from about 50% to about 40%.

Table 11-1
Discount Factors for Ironstone Inclusions in the Face of a Boulder Opal

Precious Opal as % of Face	Discount Factor
100%	0.00
95% to Under 100%	-0.30
90% to Under 95%	-0.50
70% to Under 90%	-0.60
50% to Under 70%	-0.80
10% to Under 50%	-0.90
Less than 10%	-1.50

Example

To see how these adjustments work, let's look at an example. Suppose you were presented with a boulder opal of 8 carats. The fire is brilliant (Level 5) red multicolor on a black base color. (Chapter 5.) To expose this fire, the cutter had to carve the surface into a moderately irregular freeform. Even so, there is about 60% of the surface that is opal, the rest being ironstone. All other characteristics are good. Here is how this stone would be evaluated.

Table 11-2
Example Valuation Of A Boulder Opal

Part One:

I.   Type is <u>Boulder Opal</u>.

II.   Base color is <u>Boulder Black</u>.

III.   Quality is <u>Extra Fine</u> (brightness Level 5).

IV.   Size is <u>Medium</u>.

V.   A. The appropriate table is <u>10-6</u>, Line 1.
         B. The price range is <u>$11,000</u> to <u>$20,000</u>, Line 2.

Part Two:

I.   A. Base Price is ($11,000 + $20,000) ÷ = <u>$15,500</u>, Line 3.
         C. Spread of Price is $20,000 - $11,000 = <u>$9,000</u>, Line 4.

VII.   A & B

Characteristic	Finding	Value Addition
Fire Color	Red Multicolor	+.20
Pattern	Flashfire	.00
Dome	Moderately Irregular	-.20
Cut	Good	.00
Shape	Freeform	-.20
Inclusions	60% opal face	-.80
Cracks	None	.00
Consistency	Consistent	.00
Directionality	Slightly	.00
Size	Medium	<u>.00</u>

         C. Total Value Addition   <u>-1.00</u>, Line 5

VIII.   Base Price Adjustment <u>$9,000</u> x <u>-1.00</u> = -<u>$9,000</u>, Line 6
                              Line 4   Line 5

IX.   Adjusted Base Price <u>$15,500</u> - <u>$9,000</u> = <u>$6,500</u>, Line 7
                             Line 3   Line 6

X.   Total Estimated Price:
                 (Line 7 = Line 8 for boulder opal) $6,500.00

XI.   A review finds this price appropriate.

Referring to Table 11-2, we can follow the evaluation.

The type is boulder black of a medium size, so we use Table 10-6 unadjusted. (Adjustment for non-black base color boulder opals will be discussed shortly.) A brightness level of 5 classifies the stone as Extra Fine. The price range for such stones is $11,000 to $20,000 each.

In Part Two, note the special adjustments for dome and inclusions. These cause a substantial reduction in the value of this opal. Still, after these adjustments the opal has a value of $6,500. This boulder black opal is beautiful in spite of these inclusions so the price is justified.

There are people who will say *The Guide* is crazy. "A boulder opal at $80,000? Ridiculous! They never sell for over $500 or $1,000 per stone!" But they do. These extraordinary stones are rare to be sure. Yet they exist and are sold readily when found. A look at Photographs 11-9 through 11-12 will tell you why. They are extraordinary examples of boulder opal. Beautiful boulders that sell for $5,000 to $10,000 each, while more common in the United States market, are still rare.

The "Three Sisters" and "Sydney By Night," Photographs 8-19 and 8-20 used as examples of picture stones, are both boulder opals. The interesting boulder opals in Photograph 11-9 contain faces, indeed a whole scene in the one on the left. While picture scenes are rare even in boulder opal, you stand a better chance of finding one in a boulder than in other types of opal.

Other Boulder Opals

Boulder opals that do not face black, while very attractive, are considerably less valuable than boulder blacks, all other things being equal. Of course, they never are. The value of a boulder opal, as distinct from a boulder black, follows the same rules and percentages but from a much lower base price. A simple approximation that works well most of the time is to value a crystal or semi-crystal on brown boulder at *half* a boulder black, and value a boulder with opaque opal (white, gray or orange) at *one-third* the black boulder price. All other deductions remain the same. To make this correction, mark the base color in Section II of the Opal

Beautiful Boulder Black Opals

Photograph 11-9   *Rudy G. Weber*

Photograph 11-10   *Len Cram*

Beautiful Boulder Black Opals

Photograph 11-11   *Rudy G. Weber*

Photograph 11-12   *Rudy G. Weber*

Evaluation Form as Boulder Brown or Boulder White and reduce the Price Range (Line 2) by either 50% for the Boulder Brown or 67% for the Boulder White.

The patterns in boulder opal include all the common patterns found in other types of opal. The pattern in Photograph 11-4 is a flashfire. The red stone in Photograph 11-6 is a broad flashfire. In addition to the common patterns, ribbon and striped patterns as in Photograph 11-10 are found fairly frequently. Also, picture patterns are more frequent in boulder than in other opals.

Split Face Boulder: Not many split face boulder opals are produced. The miner or cutter is taking a big chance that they will ruin a valuable stone. Consequently, when a beautiful split face like Photograph 11-13 is found, it sells for a premium over the price that would be paid for each piece individually. The premium ranges from 20% to 40% depending upon the attractiveness of the pair. They can be real treasures. This premium can be added to the Price Range (Line 2) of the Opal Evaluation Form.

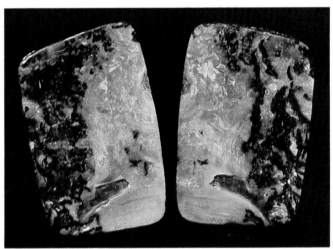

Photograph 11-13   *Rudy G. Weber*
Split Face Boulder Opal

Boulder Matrix: Boulder matrix is a mixture of opal and ironstone, but it is different from the boulder opal in seams that we have previously discussed. In this form of boulder opal the precious opal is mixed through the ironstone, not just in thin seams. In some stones the opal appears in patches or blobs, in others it appears as thin lines. Photograph 11-14 is an example of the patch type and Photograph 11-15 is an example of the Yowah line type. The most popular matrix location is Yowah in southwestern Queensland. This area produces some very unique and attractive patterns. Mainside is the other well known matrix area. There are many more.

Photograph 11-14   *Rudy G. Weber*

Boulder matrix, like other boulder opal, comes in black, crystal on brown, and white. A true black look is quite rare. The most common form is crystal on brown.

Boulder matrix is valued about half regular boulder opal.

The value of boulder matrix depends upon the usual considerations of any boulder opal. Except when the pattern is particularly attractive as in Photograph 11-15, then a premium is added for the pattern. This premium, added on the pattern line of Section VII of the Opal Evaluation Form could run from 10% to 40%. Some boulder matrix faces as black opal. Then use Table 10-6 unadjusted, still taking into account percentage of opal, brightness, etc. and adjusting for pattern. Most boulder matrix is crystal on brown. In this case, divide the estimated price from Table 10-6 in half as you would for regular boulder while still having adjusted for pattern (and percentage of opal on face). Enter the reduced values for Price Range on Line 2 of the Opal Evaluation Form.

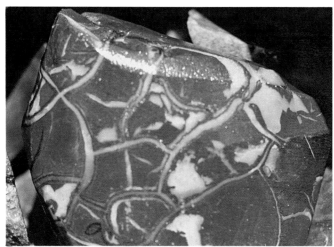

Photograph 11-15 *Len Cram*

On occasion the Yowah opals have a pure crystal center such as Photograph 11-16. These Yowahs sell at a premium when the crystal is really top grade brilliant material. The rarest of all is a Yowah with an attractive pattern of red fire on a boulder black base

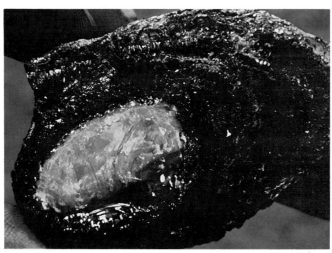

Photograph 11-16 *Len Cram*

surrounding a center of red black crystal. I have only seen one and it was not for sale, so I have no idea what such a piece would cost. It was stunning!

Andamooka Boulder

Another type of boulder opal is found in the Andamooka mining area of South Australia. This consists of seams of crystal opal in a tan quartzite. It is rarely cut into jewelry pieces. Instead, it is sold as specimens. It became traditional for local Andamooka artists to paint scenes on top of the exposed seams of opal, using the opal as part of the scene. They became known as *Painted Ladies*. Painted ladies are not widely available. Consequently they do not have established prices. With the exception of a few rare pieces, they are sold to tourists as a memento of their trip to the Outback.

Conclusions

Boulder opal is much more difficult to value than other opals. This is because of the rapid price increases that have occurred in the 1980s. Prices continue to soar in the 1990s without any evidence of an end.

Boulder opal is differentiated from boulder matrix. Within boulder opal are boulder black, crystal and semi-crystal on brown boulder, as well as opaque boulder. The boulder black carries the highest price with crystal being about one-half its price, and white being about one-third its price.

Boulder matrix is valued like other boulders with deductions for ironstone inclusions in the face and irregular carved faces. In addition, special attention and a premium is paid for the attractive patterns found in the Yowah opal.

Review

1.   The best boulder black opal can rival black opals in beauty.

2. As a general rule, boulder blacks are about one-third the price of solid blacks.

3. The lighter boulder opals with crystal or semi-crystal faces are valued at about one-half the boulder blacks, while the white and other opaque boulder opals are valued at about one-third boulder blacks.

4. There are major deductions in the price of all boulder opals for ironstone inclusions in the face of the stone.

5. Boulder matrix is valued like other boulder except for special attention paid to the unique and attractive patterns found in Yowah opal.

6. The rapid rise in popularity and the resultant unsettled, though rapidly rising market for boulder opal, make it more difficult to value than other opals.

Photograph 11-17   *Rudy G. Weber*

Chapter 12

Mexican Opal Values

Opal is found all over the world. While Australia is by far the most important source for quality gem opal, there are many other sources you may come in contact with from time to time. Mexico is the second most important source of jewelry opal. Even though Mexican opal is noted for its clear orange base color, there are many different base colors found there.

Let me make one important point. It is the characteristics of the opal, not its origin, that determine the market value. The reason for discussing opal specifically by source is to explain how the characteristics found in these opals fit into the general pricing scheme outlined in Chapter 10.

Mexican Opal

A crisp reddish-orange color permeates the stone you hold in your hand. From within come brilliant flashes of red, yellow and green fire, seemingly floating in the transparent medium. As the opal is turned, the colors move through the stone as if suspended in liquid. This magnificent stone is a top quality Mexican opal.

When one thinks of Mexican opal, it is this reddish-orange color and transparency that come to mind. While it is the most prized base color, it is by no means the only base color found in the

Mexican material. Mexican opal can have a water clear base, any degree of yellow to orange to deep red-brown, white, and very rarely seen black.[29] There are even recent finds of blue base color opals in northern Mexico. The best Mexican opals are crystal clear, but semi-crystal and opaque (equivalent to Coober Pedy white base) opals are found. Thus, they cover the full range that is found in Australian opal. (Yes, there are a few orange base color opals found in Australia.) The complete range of characteristics of Mexican opals is listed in Table 12-1.

Table 12-1
Range of Characteristics of Mexican Opal

Type	Solid or boulder (opal in rhyolite)
Base Color	White, yellow, orange, red, black
Clarity	Opaque, semi-crystal, crystal
Fire Color	All colors or lacking play of color
Treatments	Some dyed black by smoking[30]

When valuing solid Mexican opals, it is necessary to distinguish three types. There are the clear orange crystal opals with play of color that are the best that Mexico has to offer. Let us call these *precious orange crystal* opals. Then there are the translucent to opaque orange to white base stones with play of color. We will call these *precious translucent orange* opals. Finally, there are clear orange base color opals with no play of color. These stones are typically faceted rather than cabbed. While the industry calls these opals *fire opal*, as stated in Chapter 5, this leads to great confusion. I believe the time has come to change the name to *orange opals*.

---

[29]"Black Cat's-eye Opal from Jalisco, Mexico," *Gems & Gemology*, Winter, 1990, p. 304.

[30]R. Kammerling, J. Koivula, and R. Kane "Gemstone Enhancement and its Detection in the 1980s," *Gems & Gemology*, Spring, 1990, p. 34.

Precious Orange Crystal

The prices for these stones follow closely those for other crystal opals. Thus, use the Crystal Opal Table (Table 10-3) to obtain a value. Adjust per Table 10-7 just as you would for any other crystal opal with one addition. Differences in the base color can affect the price considerably. In the Opal Evaluation Form, add a line to Section III which is for orange base color. Adjust according to Table 12-2. Then add to obtain Total Additions or Subtractions (Line 5). Also note that opaque centers or edges are found in otherwise clear orange stones.[31] This opaqueness often spreads over time and is a sign that the opal has a tendency to dry out and become totally opaque and/or to craze. Adjust value accordingly. Otherwise proceed as per the instructions in Chapter 10, including the quality guidelines contained in Section III of the Opal Evaluation Form.

Table 12-2
Value Adjustments For Precious Orange Crystal

Base Color	Value Addition or Subtraction
Water Clear	-.20
Light Yellow	-.40
Yellow	-.30
Yellow-Orange	-.20
Orange	-.10
Reddish-Orange	.00
Red	-.05
Dark Red	-.15
Red-Brown	-.30

[31]"Opals with an Unusual Inclusion," *Gems & Gemology*, Fall, 1990, p. 222.

Clearly it can be seen in Table 12-2 that the most preferred base color is the reddish-orange. When the opal is transparent and the hue is just right, this color has a life all its own. Dark reds interfere with the red fire in the stone, rendering it less attractive. The red-brown base color begins to look dirty and thus less attractive.

Water clear opals (those that have no base color) are very attractive if the density of the play of color is high. However, most of the water clear crystal from Mexico lacks density in its fire color. If the stone you are evaluating lacks density in its play of color, whether water clear or with one of the other base colors, a negative adjustment of -.10 to -.30 should be made on the consistency line in Section VII of the Opal Evaluation Form.[32]

It is useful to note that some precious orange crystal opal is faceted rather than cabbed. The evaluation of such opals proceeds as above with no premium or deduction for the fact that the stone is faceted. However, the quality of cut is assessed as you would any other faceted stone. Look for the appropriate angles of facets, the meeting of facets, etc.

A word about prices of top stones is appropriate here. The truly top precious orange crystal opals will command these top prices. However, Extra Fine grade opals from Mexico are truly rare and very seldom seen in the United States. Thus, most stones will fit into the three lower grades.

Precious Translucent Orange

The translucent to opaque orange base precious opals generally fit into the same price range as Australian white base opals (Table 10-5). Again, a base color adjustment is necessary as above (Section VII). Otherwise valuation proceeds as explained in Chapter 10. Likewise white base opaque opals from Mexico are evaluated as if they were Australian white base stones.

---

[32]Density of the play of color refers to how much of the opal shows color flashes at any one orientation. Low density of fire implies that the stone has large gaps between the chunks of fire.

Valuing Non-Precious Orange Opal

Orange base clear opal without a play of color is typically faceted. It is commonly called Fire Opal but I believe it should just be called *Orange Faceted Opal*. This opal follows a different price structure from precious opal. This price structure is presented in Table 12-3.

Table 12-3
Orange Opal (Fire Opal)
Reddish-Orange Faceted Grade
Retail Price Per Carat

	Commercial	Good	Fine	Extra Fine
1 to under 5 ct	6-40	40-80	80-120	120-200
5 to under 10 ct	10-50	50-100	100-150	150-300

Source: Adjusted to Retail from *The Guide*, pp. 2-7, Oct. 1991.

Here we need to discuss the meaning of the quality grades. In these faceted opals quality revolves around clarity and color, as well as the other two "Cs"; cut and carat weight. The relationship between color, clarity and quality can be found in Table 12-4. Note that only the clearest and best color (reddish-orange) fit into the highest category. After having determined the base quality of a non-precious orange faceted opal, adjustments for cut, inclusions and cracks must be made. These adjustments are much more like those for amethyst than for opal. I presume you are familiar with assessments of cut, etc. for faceted stones. But if you are not, remember that cut has much more of an effect on the value of a faceted stone than it does on a cabbed opal. Adjust accordingly.

Table 12-4
Quality Grades For Non-Precious
Orange Faceted Opals

Base Color	Clarity		
	Hazy	Clear	Very Clear
Water clear	Commercial	Commercial	Commercial
Light Yellow	Commercial	Commercial	Commercial
Yellow	Commercial	Commercial	Good
Yellow-Orange	Commercial	Good	Good
Orange	Good	Good	Fine
Reddish-Orange	Good	Fine	Extra Fine
Red	Good	Good	Fine
Dark Red	Commercial	Good	Good
Red-Brown	Commercial	Commercial	Good

Mexican Black Opal

I have been told that some true black opals have been found in Mexico. I thought I had purchased a couple such stones a few years back, but I now believe that my stones have been dyed by smoking them to make them look black. I have come to this conclusion because the stones feel sticky. That is, they tend to stick to my fingers. This sticky feeling is an indication that an opal has lost a portion of the water usually trapped between the silica spheres. Such opals are called hydrophane opals. They are porous and thus can absorb the dye. GIA has documented at least one case of natural black opal from Mexico. If an opal is represented to you as a Mexican black, it may be dyed. Have it checked by GIA. Such stones, if natural, are so rare there is no defined market price.

Mexican Blue Opal

There is a blue base color opal found in northern Mexico. It appears identical to material found in Arizona and up into lower Idaho, so its evaluation will be covered in the section on United States opal in the next chapter.

Contra Luz Opal

Some Mexican opals show a play of color only under transmitted light. Such opals are called *contra luz* or against the light. If an opal only shows a play of color when light passes through it, it is of little value as jewelry. Judge such stones only on the fire they exhibit as they would be worn. If they show no fire as they are worn, classify them as non-precious orange opal. Sometimes contra luz stones are faceted and the transmitted light off the back facets can pick up some of the fire. Then, of course, you would value the stone as a precious orange crystal opal with the brightness of fire judged as seen from the front as you look down on the stone with your eye next to your grading light.

Mexican Boulder Opal

The opal in Mexico is found in a light to dark tan rhyolite. (See Photograph 6-8.) While the rhyolite is relatively soft, inexpensive stones are cut with an opal center and rhyolite surrounding it. The value of the finished piece depends upon the amount and quality of the opal contained within it. The better of these stones can be quite attractive. Prices for such stones range from $1 to $200 per stone (they are not sold by the carat), with a few exceptional stones going beyond this level. However, the dominant range is from $5 to $50 per stone.

A common tourist item is an egg-shaped rhyolite rock with opal inclusions. These eggs look as if they were carved from natural opal in rhyolite rock. Usually they are a clever work of man where rhyolite is mixed with glue, roughly shaped, and pieces of opal inserted on the surface. When the glue sets, the egg shape is finalized and polished. Such "opal eggs" usually sell for only a few dollars each. Other carved items, especially turtles, are made this way and again are inexpensive. However, there are some figures and eggs which are made from the natural material. These are more expensive but no more than equivalent opal and rhyolite cabs.

Summary

Mexican opal is typically an orange crystal. Grades range from a reddish-orange crystal with full brilliant multicolor to material with no play of color but an orange clear base. Other bases are found but are far less common. When valuing the orange opal an additional consideration is the color of the base. The reddish-orange is most valued with lighter and darker shades valued somewhat less. In valuing faceted opals, judge cut as you would other faceted stones.

Review

1. Mexican opal is sought after because of the reddish-orange crystal base found in the best quality. Many other base colors are found but they are less valued.

2. Orange crystal with no play of fire, which the industry inappropriately calls "Fire Opal," are usually faceted. These attractive stones vary in price depending upon base color, clarity, cut, and carat weight.

3. While natural black opal has been reported from Mexico, in 28 years I have yet to see a piece. The few "blacks" I have seen have been dyed.

4. Mexican boulder opal, opal and tan rhyolite, is found and often fashioned into inexpensive cabs and carvings.

Chapter 13

United States and Other Sources

After Mexico, the next most important sources of opal are the United States and Brazil. Other locations are Honduras, Java (Indonesia), and Hungary. Each area has unique characteristics which can affect value.

There are many sources of opal in the United States.[33] The main areas are Virgin Valley, Nevada, and Spencer, Idaho, but other types of precious opal are found in Arizona, Oregon and Louisiana. Each type has its own unique characteristics and beauty. Let us take them up in the order mentioned.

Nevada Opal

From a little valley tucked in the northwestern corner of Nevada comes some of the most spectacular opal in the world. Bright reds, greens, and blues shimmer in a dense translucent black background. Other stones have brilliant fire captured in a water clear crystal. Some have base colors that range from yellow to orange to brown. An example of this type of opal is found in Photograph 5-7. A crystal find, mined by Keith Hodson and known as the *Bonanza Opal*, produced over 8 pounds of truly top crystal. Photograph 13-1

---

[33]For more detail on the sources of American Opal, see Paul B. Downing, *Opal Adventures*, Chapter 19.

shows two pieces of this find along with Agnes Hodson's wonderful ring from this opal.

Photograph 13-1   *Keith Hodson*
Nevada Opal: Bonanza Find

With such wonderful opal available, why isn't it well known in the jewelry industry? Because, unfortunately, a large percentage of it is not stable. When taken out of water, it tends to craze. But there is a portion of the opal from Nevada that is stable. The cutable stones are, in fact, very stable. So you may see a cut opal from this source; especially since several miner/cutters are actively marketing cut Nevada opal at this time. Most Nevada opal, however, is sold uncut in glass bottles as specimens. Even these specimens can command high prices because of their stunning beauty.

The cut stones can have black to opaque orange to white to water clear base color. A word about the black stones is appropriate. Recall that the GIA definition of black opal includes brown. This is because the Nevada opal that faces as black will be brown in a thin cross-section. This is seen easily in Photograph 5-7 where the right side is brown and the left is black. These stones are true black opals even though they are a dark variety of brown rather than the dark variety of gray that forms the base color of Australian blacks.

Valuing Nevada cut stones is straightforward. The blacks are valued as you would Australian black, assuming they are stable and guaranteed for a reasonable length of time. The opaque orange to white stones would be valued as you would equivalent Mexican opals, adjusting for the orange base color as per Table 12-2. The water clear crystal would be valued as crystal, the same as you would Australian crystal; again being careful to adjust for density of fire in those examples with lower density.

Another type of Nevada opal is sometimes seen. Most Nevada opal is a replacement of wood. There are occasions where the opal has only replaced part of the wood. The rest is silicified and retains its wood graining. This combination of opal and petrified wood, called conk, produces some unique patterns. Cut stones from this opal and wood combination are uncommon but are available. The wood has been treated with a polymer because the silica is soft and tends to break apart. The opal is just fine. The cut stones are sold by the piece, not the carat. The price depends upon size, amount of opal, fire brightness, and especially the pattern. I have a bolo tie with a scene of two opal deer, one drinking and the other guarding. Prices for such pieces range from $50 to $500 or more.

Idaho Opal

This opal is found in a hard rhyolite. Typically it is formed in thin straight lines of precious crystal opal contained in a white potch. While there are a few stones that are cut as solids, most of this material is cut into triplets or doublets with a quartz cap and clear or white opal under it.[34] Thus we will leave valuing to the next chapters where we discuss valuing doublets and triplets. However, if you do encounter a solid Idaho opal, value it as you would an equivalent Australian solid opal.

Blue Opal

This unique blue base color opal was first found at the J-R Mine in Arizona but now is being found in several locations from southern Idaho to northern Mexico. Cut stones have a dense opaque

---

[34]Earl Spendlove, "Idaho Opal," *Rock & Gem*, October, 1991, p. 33-36.

wedgewood blue base color. These opals are cut as solid cabochons. Typically they have red and green fire. The brightness of the fire is generally up to Level 3 but occasionally a brighter stone is found. When valuing these stones treat them as if they were white base Australian opals.

Oregon Opal

Precious opal has been discovered in Oregon. This material can be blue or clear and translucent to transparent. Thus when it contains a play of color this opal would be classified as a blue or clear crystal.[35] There is too little market experience with this material to know whether it will sell at a premium or discount as compared to the clear crystal from Australia. In the absence of any more market information, I would suggest that you value it as you would other crystal opal. Some of this opal, like some Mexican opal, has *contra luz* fire. Remember that it is only the fire that shows as the stone is worn that counts for valuing the opal. A stone that you have to hold up to the light to see the fire has value only as a specimen. (This is not to suggest that such specimens will necessarily be inexpensive.) There is also an opal found here which Mr. Smith calls "Rainbow Opal." It has "iridescent soft hues of different colors but no play of color as light passes through it." While Mr. Smith classifies this rainbow opal as precious opal, if it does not have a distinct pattern and play of color, the opal industry would not call it precious. Still it is quite attractive.

Louisiana Opal

The opal found in Louisiana is a matrix type opal. It is found in a grayish quartzite. It is similar in some ways to Andamooka matrix but harder and does not appear to be porous enough to take a treatment, so it cannot be dyed. It is found in massive chunks of quartzite, usually containing a smaller portion of precious opals. The fire is typically blue and green with occasional orange and red fire pieces. There are a lot of surface pits and dark inclusions in most of

---

[35]Kevin Lane Smith, "Opals from Opal Butte, Oregon," *Gems & Gemology*, Winter, 1988, pp. 229-236.

Photograph 13-2   *Keith Griffin*

it. Photograph 13-2 shows a nice example of a Louisiana matrix opal with a blue gray background and red and green fire. Again there is very little market experience with this material. People have claimed to have sold some of the better pieces at $50 per carat or more. Most material appears to sell for $5 to $20 per carat, primarily because of the novelty of this source. But there is no real established market for this material. It is all mined and sold by one organization.

Brazilian Opal

Brazil has produced opal for many years. During the mid- to late- 1970s a large volume of rough from Brazil was brought to the United States. Since then it is seldom seen in rough form. Brazilian opal has the full range of base colors but most of it is semi-crystal and crystal. A recent find of natural black opal has been reported. Some of this material is rather porous and has been treated with *Opticon.*[36] I have not seen any yet. Be careful here because another type of Brazilian opal called hydrophane has been treated with black epoxy or other polymers to simulate black opal.[37] It is

[36]"Black Opal From Brazil," *Gems & Gemology*, Spring, 1991, p. 49.

[37]Personal communication with John Slocum, October, 1990.

difficult to distinguish treated from natural stones without laboratory tests. Brazilian opal is a bit harder than Australian opal. Some claim a hardness of 7 for Brazilian opal instead of 5.5 to 6.5 for the Australian material.

When cut, most Brazilian opal is almost impossible to distinguish from Australian opal. In fact, it is rumored that most Brazilian opal is sent to Australia, cut, and sold as Australian opal. This tells us exactly how to treat it for valuing. If it is interchangeable with Australian opal, it will command the same prices. Thus, value it just as you would any equivalent Australian opal, as per Chapter 10.

Java Opal

The opal from the Java area of Indonesia looks very similar to Nevada opal. The blacks are brown in thin cross-sections. Many stones are opaque brownish orange. Typically, like the Nevada material, the cut stones are small, less than 3 carats, although there are exceptions. Not much of this material reaches the United States market. It would be valued in the same way Nevada and Mexican opal is valued.

Honduras Opal

The most familiar opal from Honduras is the matrix opal where small pinfire flecks of fire spread throughout a black basalt.[38] (See Photograph 13-3.) In essence, the basalt is like the ironstone in Queensland matrix, except it is black and weighs much less. The basalt is softer than the opal. When polished, it shows its porous nature. Gray inclusions may be scattered throughout the surface. Most of what you see in the market is relatively low quality material with no more than Level 3 brightness. This material seldom sells for over $20 per carat. There are, as in almost any material, exceptional pieces which can sell for $50 to $100 per carat or more,

---

[38]For a full discussion of Honduras Opal, see Paul B. Downing, *Opal Adventures*, Chapter 19 and Tony Dabdoub *Opal Report From Honduras* (Tropical Gem Explorations, 1985).

Honduras Matrix
Black Doublet

Photograph 13-3   *Tony Dabdoub*

Seam Opal in
Dark Matrix from
Honduras

Photograph 13-4   *Tony Dabdoub*

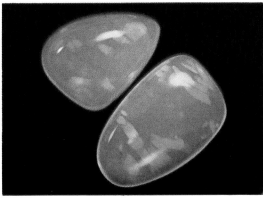

Crystal Opal
from Honduras

Photograph 13-5   *Tony Dabdoub*

but they are very rare. Sometimes the basalt is treated with polymers to strengthen it and make it take a better polish. NOTE: This is not black opal. It is technically a boulder matrix.

Another Honduras opal consists of thin lines of crystal opal in the dark matrix. These are just like Queensland boulder opal in structure and treatment. They are cut by following the lines of color almost as if they are carved. When these thin lines of top gem red crystal are set against the dark matrix they can be breathtaking. (See Photograph 13-4.) They are also extremely rare. Thus, pricing is a real problem. However, it is reasonable to treat them as you would a boulder black.

Even more rare is a Honduras opal that is water clear with brilliant fire. It is found in small nodules and is rarely stable when cut. However, those stones that are stable are true gems and would be valued as crystal opal in Chapter 10. (See Photograph 13-5.) More frequently this clear opal is made into triplets. These triplets would be valued like other triplets as discussed in Chapter 15.

Hungarian Opal

Rarely seen nowadays, the opal that the Romans highly prized and the stone the Australian opal was compared to when it first appeared in London was from Hungary. The only piece I have seen that I know, with relative certainty, is from this source is on display at the Smithsonian. It is a white base with red multicolor fire of brightness Level 3. It would present quite a contrast to the brilliant red crystal that T. C. Wollaston brought from Queensland and introduced to the London market in the late 1890s. (See *Opal Adventures*, Chapter 2.)

Modern production of Hungarian opal has ceased because the material now found is unstable and does not compete with the Australian opal. So if you run into a Hungarian opal it is likely to be in an old pre-1900 piece of jewelry. There is no defined market value for such stones as there is no market—they are too rare. All you can do is estimate the value of an equivalent Australian opal. Again, it is almost impossible to determine origin so the stone you see in that old piece may be a 1920s replacement from Australia. Thus, placing a rarity value on it is hazardous.

Summary

While Australia produces the vast majority of the world's jewelry opal, some outstanding stones are found in other locations.

United States opal sources are many and varied. The oldest source is the Virgin Valley area of Nevada. It produces all ranges of opals from black to orange to crystal, but only a small percentage is cutable.

Idaho opal is rarely cut as solid opal. Most are made into triplets. Blue opal is fairly rare but may become more common as the new finds of the past two years start to reach production. It is valued similar to white base Australian opal.

Brazilian opal is usually indistinguishable from Australian opal once cut. Java, Honduras and Hungary also produce precious opal but these opals are rarely seen in the United States market.

In general, opal is valued independent of its source. However, orange, brown and blue base colors are seldom found in Australia but are found in other locations. Thus adjustments must be made to reflect how these base colors affect value. With this exception, it is a general rule to ignore source and to value based upon the opal's characteristics.

Review

1. Opal is valued based upon its characteristics, not its source. However, the United States and other sources produce base colors not commonly found in Australian opal.

2. Nevada and Java opal produces a black opal which is brown in thin sections. This opal is valued as black opal if it faces black.

3. Brazilian opal is usually indistinguishable from Australian opal and is valued as if it were Australian.

4. Honduras produces many types of opal but the one most commonly found in the market is a matrix opal with pinfire in black basalt.

5. Hungarian opal looks like white base Australian opal and is valued accordingly, though rarely seen now.

Beautiful Opal Doublets

Photograph 14-1   *Walch & Williams*

Chapter 14

Doublets

You will recall from Chapter 3 that doublets are two-part stones. Usually the precious opal forms the face of the stone and another material, usually black potch, ironstone, or black jade, is used to back the precious opal. Sometimes, though rarely, doublets are made by gluing a quartz cap on top of a slice of opal. Triplets are three-part stones with a thin opal slice glued between a clear cap and dark back. Typically both doublets and triplets are made with a dark back to intensify the fire and give the appearance of a black opal. We will cover triplets in the next chapter.

Valuing Doublets

Just the other day I received a beautiful photograph from one of my customers. He produces high dome doublets using black jade as the backing for the stone. The picture, reproduced as Photograph 14-1, reminded me how beautiful a well made doublet can be. It is clear to see from this picture why doublets are popular.

There are three main reasons for making doublets. Doublets can use pieces of opal that may be too thin to cut solid stones. By making a doublet you can save some beautiful material that would otherwise be lost. Doublets are darkened on the back so that they look like natural black opals from the top. Since they use less expensive, though not necessarily cheap, crystal opal, a doublet allows one to have the look of a black opal at a fraction of the price.

Doublets, if cut correctly and especially if backed with black jade, are as tough or tougher than natural opals of equivalent dimensions.

In valuing a doublet, the same steps are used as for a solid stone. Initially the type is determined. There are two general types of doublets. One type has an appearance like natural solid stones such as blacks, semi-blacks or crystal opals. These are just called *Doublets* in the trade. Sometimes they are termed Black Opal Doublets to imply that they are more valuable or look like black opal. This, however, is incorrect terminology since it does not fit the accepted definition of black opal. Refer to them only as doublets, not black doublets. The other type are doublets backed with ironstone to give the appearance of natural boulder black opals. They are usually termed *Boulder Doublets*. Sometimes they are referred to as *Shell Doublets* because the precious opal is derived from thin clam shells found in Coober Pedy. (See Chapter 3.)

Regular Doublets

Let us first discuss the valuing of regular doublets, those that look like natural solid stones. All the characteristics of the stone are assessed in the same fashion as outlined in the Opal Evaluation Form in Chapter 10. However, there are two characteristics which must be even more carefully analyzed than normally.

> ## Cut is especially important in evaluating a doublet.

Cut is one of the most important areas for examination in a doublet. Doublets may be cut as high, medium, or low-dome pieces. (See Figure 14-1.) The thickness of the dome is important because high-domed doublets are strong, while low-dome doublets are very brittle. The thin edge of a low-domed (sometimes flat) doublet can, and often does, chip. Looking at the cross section of the low-domed doublet in Figure 14-1, it is easy to see why the precious opal on the top of these stones chips and cracks along the edge. On the other hand, a nice high-dome doublet has plenty of precious opal "meat" to hold the stone together. Such well cut doublets seldom crack.

Another problem in cut for doublets can be seen at the right of Figure 14-1. If you looked at this stone from above, a dark ring of non-precious material would be evident around the opal. Not very attractive. Also, this shape produces a thin edge. While not as vulnerable as the flat top doublet to its left, it is still prone to chipping.

Figure 14-1

Cuts in Doublets

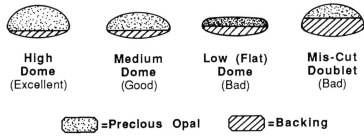

| High Dome (Excellent) | Medium Dome (Good) | Low (Flat) Dome (Bad) | Mis-Cut Doublet (Bad) |

=Precious Opal   =Backing

From this discussion, it should be clear that when you get to the assessment of cut in Section VII of the Opal Evaluation Form, some special attention must be paid to the dome of the doublet. If a stone must be cut as a thin flat topped stone, it should be made into a triplet because it will not hold up as a doublet. A fairly thick shoulder is required for structural integrity in a doublet.

The next element of cut is the backing used in making the doublet. The tradition in Australia is to back doublets with natural black potch. This makes the stones look as close to natural blacks as possible. One of my close friends, Ted Priester of Lightning Ridge, is a master at cutting these doublets. The finished product is almost indistinguishable from a natural stone (except for the straight line and glue visible under magnification). (See Chapter 4.) Furthermore, with his careful construction, these doublets are as tough or tougher than natural stones. Others are equally careful, so well cut doublets with an opal backing will last a long time.

Table 14-1
Value Additions or Subtractions for Doublets

Dome	Addition or Subtraction
High	.00
Medium	-.10
Low	-.75

Backing	Addition or Subtraction
Opal Potch	.00
Black Jade	+.20
Onyx or other soft material	-.20

NOTE: Enter the sum of these two and any other elements of cut into Line 7 of the Opal Evaluation Form.

In the United States many different materials are used to back doublets. By far the best is black jade. This tough material strengthens the doublet considerably. Years ago I made a jade backed doublet. At least 10 years later I made a ring for my wife, Bobbi, using this stone. One day while moving a set of collapsible bleachers they collapsed on her finger. The ring was crushed. It took us a half hour working with pliers to get the ring off her finger. The gold was a mess, but the doublet (and her finger) was, and still is, just fine. The jade saved the opal.

On the other hand, many United States cutters use various types of soft material to back doublets, the most common being onyx and basanite. These softer backs do not strengthen the opal and, in some cases, they break before the opal does. Thus, these soft backings reduce the value of a doublet.

To evaluate a doublet, value the opal as if it were a solid stone. If it faces up as a black, value it as a black. The only difference is the adjustment for cut listed in Table 14-1. Once you have determined the total value of the solid stone equivalent of the doublet, including adjustments for base and cut, take *one-tenth* of its value as the market value of the doublet. This is the rule of thumb used in Lightning Ridge.

> **A doublet is worth one-tenth
> the value of an
> equivalent solid opal.**

This sounds way too low, but it works out. Remember that most doublets face as black or semi-black opals. Suppose a doublet with a nice high dome values at $20,000 if it were a solid black opal. The value of the doublet would be $2,000. Stated another way, if a natural stone were worth $2,500 per carat, the equivalent doublet would be worth $250 per carat.

This is not to suggest that all doublets are valued this highly. A flat topped doublet with dull fire (Level 2) and a grayish cast would be valued at $1 per carat or less.

Boulder Doublets

Boulder doublets would be valued the same way. Assess the doublet as if it were a solid boulder opal using Table 10-6, and adjust if the doublet does not face with a black base color. Pay particular attention to whether there is a thin edge of precious opal that may be easily broken. If there is, adjust accordingly using Table 14-1. Also, the ironstone should not be too thin, as it becomes brittle. Value the base as you would an opal base (no deduction). Once the total value of the natural stone equivalent is determined, one-tenth of this value would be the market value of the boulder doublet.

Other Forms of Doublets

There are two other forms of doublets that are produced commercially in the Orient. Inexpensive gold plated jewelry is being made using small pieces of opal fit together. These are called *Mosaics*. Usually these mosaics consist of very thin sheets of opal glued to a black background, often onyx or glass. Sometimes, the mosaic work is fit inside a shallow hollowed out area. In either case,

Photograph 14-2   *Walch & Williams*

*Design and beauty make this doublet opal pendant
a magnificent example of the jeweler's art.*

the top is cut flat and polished. Because the opal is very thin, these mosaics are *very* brittle and will break. Some manufacturers have added a polymer coating or a thin layer of glass over the opal to protect it. Technically, when the covering is added they become triplets. In any case, these commercial high volume mosaics are very inexpensive. Prices for these items range from $5 to $50 depending on size, quality of opal, etc.

Occasionally a special hand created mosaic will be seen. Such pieces are much more carefully done and much more attractive than the high volume commercial mosaics discussed above. In judging value pay particular attention to how the pieces of opal fit together. The other characteristics mentioned for doublets should be weighed as well, especially the thickness and vulnerability of the opal. Note that these special mosaics will generally use small pieces of opal. Thus, regardless of the weight of the piece, use the lowest carat size in the appropriate table for valuing. Also, feel free to adjust value up or down for the artistic merit of the piece.

I am reminded here of a mosaic watch face I saw once. The pieces of opal were perfectly matched to form several interlocking chain-like patterns of different fire color combinations. Wonderful. If it had not been mounted in a $15,000 18kt gold and diamond watch, I would have bought it.

Other opal items that are technically doublets are the opal cameos glued to black onyx or glass (yes, black glass) backings done in volume in Hong Kong. The range in quality in these cameos is quite large. Frequently these cameos are machine cut, not hand carved as they were a few years ago. Quality has improved but uniqueness has been lost in these high volume machine cut cameos. They must be evaluated as opal doublets and as works of art. Prices for machine cut and hand carved backed opal cameos can range from a few dollars to several hundred dollars. Note that these are different from the free-standing all opal cameos discussed in Chapter 16.

Summary

Doublets can be beautiful and functional substitutes for black opals if they are cut with a high dome and constructed carefully. As a general rule, such well constructed doublets are valued at about one-tenth the value of equivalent natural stones.

Review

1. Doublets, if cut with a high-dome and constructed carefully, can be a beautiful and functional alternative to natural black opals.

2. As a general rule, high quality doublets are valued at about one-tenth the value of an equivalent natural stone.

3. Doublets are valued using the same procedures used for natural stones with some modifications. Particular attention must be paid to *cut* and *backing*.

4. Cut is particularly important in doublets. A high-dome and a thick shoulder produce a tough stone. A thin stone is very fragile and very low in price.

5. Boulder doublets are valued at one-tenth the value of an equivalent natural boulder opal.

Chapter 15

Triplets, Synthetics, Simulants, and Dyed Opals

Triplets are very much different from doublets, both in their make-up and in their market value. Triplets use much less opal than high-dome doublets. Sometimes as little as one-tenth. They also use lower quality opal in most cases. Their backs are made of almost any material. At the moment, several commercial triplet manufacturers in Australia are using either glass microscope slides or ceramic tile painted black. The clear cap that distinguishes triplets from doublets can be made of any clear material. Quartz is traditional, but glass is cheaper and thus more common in recent times among commercial manufacturers.

Synthetics are now being more actively marketed and are more realistic than in the past. The most available simulants are Slocum stones. The Andamooka Treated Matrix is seen occasionally, but other dyed opals are fairly rare.

Triplets

Like doublets, triplets are made to look like expensive black opals. They partially succeed. When looking straight down upon a triplet, the pattern looks quite natural. But if you look at the stone on an angle, the pattern becomes distorted. Of course, when viewed from the side, the clear cap is readily visible. (See Chapter 4.)

> # It is incorrect to call a doublet or a triplet a black opal.

Unlike any other type of opal, there is a fairly well recognized grading system for triplets. They are graded as A, B, or C with pluses and minuses added for further differentiation. Some add a gem grade as well. Most triplets are cut to calibrated ovals.

The grading of triplets is not always consistent among dealers but it generally follows the rules set out in Table 15-1.

Table 15-1
The Grading of Triplets

Grade	Base Color	Brightness	Consistency of Fire and Pattern
Gem*	Dark Black	5	Excellent Special Pattern
A	Dark Black	4 - 5	Good to Excellent
B	Light Black	3 - 4	Good to Excellent
C	Semi-Black	3	Fair to Good
C-	Gray	2	Fair to Good

*Note: Gem grade triplets are usually cut freeform and/or have a special pattern like harlequin or star.

The best gem grade triplets have a dark black base color, brilliant red fire, and consistency of fire and pattern. Frequently they have a special pattern and are cut freeform, but shape or pattern alone do not make a triplet gem grade.

"A" Grade triplets are very black with brilliant red or orange-green fire that faces well from almost any direction. Triplets having less darkness of background, less brightness, and more directionality or inconsistency of fire are graded lower. It is not uncommon to see gaps in fire in the C and C- grades. In commercial cutting, anything below a C- is discarded as unsaleable. Also discarded are any triplets which show air bubbles between the cap and the opal. These air bubbles will quickly spread as the triplet is worn.

In fact, separation of the cap from the opal is a major problem for triplets. Moisture gets between the glue lines. When this

Table 15-2
Retail Prices of Triplets Per Piece

Size	A	B	C
6 x 4	3.45	2.50	1.85
7 x 5	5.75	3.65	2.00
8 x 6	10.35	6.00	2.30
10 x 8	23.00	11.50	3.20
12 x 10	34.50	22.00	6.40
14 x 10	40.00	24.00	8.00
16 x 12	55.00	27.50	11.50
18 x 13	110.00	41.00	23.00
25 x 18	---	51.50	---
30 x 22	---	69.00	---

Source: W. L. Maison Opals, Inc., August, 1991.

happens, the opal starts to look cloudy. This happens very frequently in commercially cut triplets. Once it starts, it ruins the look of the triplet and often spreads rapidly.

There is a fairly standard price list for these calibrated commercial triplets. (See Table 15-2.) Notice that the price is per piece and varies with the size of the triplet.

The commercial calibrated triplets are manufactured in volume to minimize costs. This is necessary in order to sell these triplets at the prices you see in Table 15-2. In fact, the opal the manufacturers use is sliced very thin. They use a multi-blade saw with 101 blades in two inches of length. Thus, they get approximately 50 slices out of one inch of solid opal. Triplet manufacturers produce thousands of triplets per day. You cannot expect them to last, and they usually don't.

Triplets serve a good purpose.

There are, of course, exceptions to this rule. Some non-volume cutters take great care and pride in cutting high quality triplets. When done well, triplets are much less prone to separate. The Idaho triplets are usually cut one stone at a time and are far better than the commercial triplets. They also produce more unique patterns and some brilliant fire. Some real collector items can be found in these Idaho triplets. The Idaho material will on occasion form a star. The star can be three-ray or six-ray. Such star triplets and other special gem triplets can sell for $1,500 each or more.

Triplets serve a good purpose. They allow individuals to enjoy the beauty of opal at a minimum cost. They can be very attractive.

Synthetics and Simulants

I really did not intend for this book to cover synthetics and simulants. But a few quick comments on value seem appropriate. Gilson synthetics are making a reappearance in the market. The newer ones are much more natural looking and come in black, white, crystal and orange base colors. (Photograph 15-1.) Prices vary somewhat between the different colors, with white being the cheapest and black the most expensive. The range in price is $120 to $220 per carat. There is little variation in quality so all price variation is by base color.[39]

Photograph 15-1   Manning International
Gilson Opal

Also seen on the market are synthetic opal triplets. They use clear Gilson opal to create unbelievably bright triplets. In fact, they are so bright they do not look real. Both calibrated and freeform synthetic triplets are available in the market. They are priced like A Grade triplets.

By far the most common simulant seen in the United States is the Slocum Stone. The Slocum Stone is not being actively marketed at the moment. However, there are some manufacturing jewelers using the stone. John Slocum tells me that prices vary with quality but a typical piece would be priced retail at $15 to $30 per carat.[40] Exceptional pieces can be priced far higher. (See Photograph 15-2.)

---

[39]Personal communication with Gerry Manning, owner of Manning Opals, the distributor for Gilson opal, October 1, 1991.

[40]Personal communication with John Slocum, the creator of Slocum Stones, September 26, 1991.

Photograph 15-2   *John Slocum*
Slocum Stones

Another simulant seen in the market is the plastic material made in Hong Kong. Usually it is set in very inexpensive gold plated findings selling for $20 to $30, although there may be exceptions here too.

Photograph 15-3   *Gerald Pauley*
An attractive opal simulant named
"Le Papillon Simulated Opal."

Plastic or resin simulants have not played an important role in the United States market in recent years. However, that may change shortly. An Australian company has developed a simulant of black opal that is very attractive and practical, yet inexpensive. They have scanned dozens of opal patterns into a computer. Using these patterns, the computer generates a limitless supply of patterns so no two simulants are exactly the same. Colors are created by dyes suspended in resin to give the pattern a depth. As the stone is moved there is an iridescent play of color. However, the pattern does not change as it would in a natural opal. Looking at this simulant from the side, the layer of dye is apparent. The resin body is, of course, much softer than a true opal.

The result, called *"Le Papillon Simulated Opal"* is quite convincing, as you can see from Photograph 15-3. Attractive gold-plated jewelry is being made and test marketed at this writing. Market prices have yet to be established.[41]

Dyed Matrix

The Andamooka treated matrix is dyed to look like black opal. (See Photographs 3-6, 4-4, and 4-5.) Again, it is incorrect to call such stones black *unless* they are naturally black—a rarity. Then they would be called black matrix, not black opal, as they are a mixture of opal and quartz similar in principle to boulder matrix. Like doublets and triplets, the value of a dyed matrix piece varies with the degree of darkness of the dyed background, the range of colors, the brightness of fire, and all the other common character-istics we have discussed. Good quality dyed matrix stones sell for $5 to $15 per carat. Fine quality for $15 to $30 per carat, and very fine quality for up to $50 per carat. I have seen one parcel of exceptional dyed matrix with brilliant red fire on a dense black background that was being offered for $100 per carat. It was in a store in Coober Pedy and we could see the opal in the display from our car over 50 yards away. It was far superior to any dyed matrix I had seen in 27 years of looking and approached the look of natural black opal.

The dyed hydrophane opal from Mexico and Brazil is so rare in the market that there is no generally recognized price. If I were to be asked to value it, I would place it in the dyed matrix category.

---

[41]Information provided by the inventor, Gerald Pauley, The Australian Gem Exchange Pty. Ltd., Australia.

Summary

Triplets are stones made by man using natural opal (and occasionally synthetic opal). They are constructed to give the appearance of black opal. However, it is not correct to call them *black opal triplets*. The term *black opal* is reserved only for stones which derive their black base color from their natural structure, not from paint and glue.

Commercially made triplets are generally very inexpensive and, because of their wearability problems, are usually not considered quality gems. Because of their low price they do provide a very inexpensive way for consumers to enjoy the beauty of opal. There are some rare triplets, such as the Idaho star opals, which command gem prices.

Synthetic opal is being heavily marketed at this writing. The new versions are difficult to distinguish from natural opals. Prices range from $120 to $220 per carat.

Dyed opals are generally inexpensive. Prices range from $5 to $50 per carat, although there may be rare examples outside this range.

Review

1. Triplets are generally low in price due to their inexpensive construction. Unfortunately, they tend not to hold up in use. Still, they serve a purpose.

2. There is a fairly standard grading for triplets ranging from a high of A to a low of C-. Some people add a gem grade above A.

3. Triplet prices vary with grade and size.

4. Synthetic opals sell generally for $120 to $220 per carat.

5. Dyed matrix and other dyed opals are graded by the common list of characteristics. Usually prices for dyed matrix are from $5 to $50 per carat.

Chapter 16

Opal Works of Art

There are many ways opal can be used in works of art. Perhaps the most common form is in carvings. Solid opal carvings and cameos have been done. Another form which is growing rapidly in popularity is *intarsia* which combines opal and other gemstones into pieces for jewelry or gemstone boxes. Mosaic pictures are another opal art form. Bronze or silver sculptures have been combined with chunks of opal to produce attractive scenes. Finally, large chunks of matrix and opal have been painted with scenes, using the opal as the background. All these art forms have value as art in addition to their opal value.

Intarsia

Intarsias are becoming very popular. And why not. A well-done intarsia is a true work of art. Intarsia jewelry pieces can be made from any materials, but some of the best feature opal, usually as the center stone. (I admit to no bias here.) Other materials commonly used are lapis, malachite, sugalite, rhodochrosite, turquoise and coral, with many other materials being used less frequently. The various materials are carefully fitted together to form a geometric pattern. A backing stone of one solid material is used to strengthen, protect, and finish the piece. Because of this backing, the opal in these pieces is technically a doublet. Photograph 16-1 shows some excellent workmanship by Jim Kaufmann.

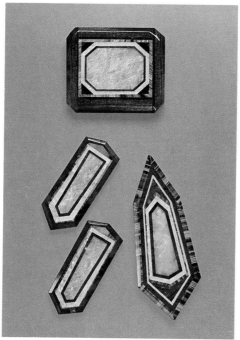

Photograph 16-1   Tino Hammid
Jim Kaufmann's Excellent
Intarsia Pendants

Valuing intarsias is very different from valuing opals and is really outside the scope of this book. They are true works of art, judged and valued more on design and workmanship than on the quality of materials. Not that the quality of materials does not influence the value of the finished piece, for it certainly does. The valuer must pay attention to the quality of the opal as well. It is how the materials compliment the design and workmanship that sets off outstanding intarsia pieces.

Pendant intarsias, such as those pictured here, use much more opal than you might imagine. A piece with 10 carats or more of opal is not unusual. The opal alone makes these pieces valuable. The workmanship and skill of the artists add to this value. Like any other work of art, individual pieces will vary widely in price. I have seen jewelry pieces for as little as $100 while some of the best jewelry pieces can be $3,000 or more, plus the setting.

Not all intarsias are crafted into jewelry. The magnificent box shown in Photograph 16-2 was made by Jim Kaufmann and won (tie) the AGTA Cutting Edge competition in 1991 for Objects d'Art.

Photograph 16-2   *Tino Hammid*

*This award-winning box by Jim Kaufmann
combines opal and other gemstones
with a magnificent 18kt gold scene.*

Mosaic Pictures

In a previous chapter I explained mosaic doublets. There is another type of commercial mosaic which is fairly common. Pendants are made to artistically render butterflies, flowers, koala bears, kangaroos and other subjects. These pendants are usually set in gold-plated findings. They are produced in an interesting way. First a mosaic doublet is produced. A design is masked off on a thin sheet of glass. The glass is then sprayed with black paint. When dry, the masking is removed, leaving the unpainted design in clear glass surrounded by black paint. Then the glass is glued to the top of the mosaic to make a mosaic triplet picture of a koala. Such commercial mosaic pictures are valued about the same as B or C Grade triplets depending on the brightness of the fire.

Occasionally, large pictures are made this same way, but they are different in that the maker usually pays particular attention to the quality of the opal. And the pictures are often one of a kind. Such special pictures can range in value from $50 to $1,000 or more, depending upon size, quality of opal, and artistic merit. They are not, however, black opal pictures as some have called them. The term *black opal* is reserved only for stones which achieve their black base color naturally.

Carvings

Opal carvings can be wonderful expressions of an artist's talents. In an exceptional carving, the artist uses the play of color to blend with the design. The petal of a flower will have a special splash of fire oriented just right. A fish will flash color on its side. Fire and matrix or potch will be played against one another to accentuate design. I often wonder how the artist knows the material will work like that.

Carvings can be done for jewelry or for exhibition only. (See Photographs 16-3 and 16-4.) All types of opal are used: solid black, gray, or white, boulder opal and treated matrix opal.

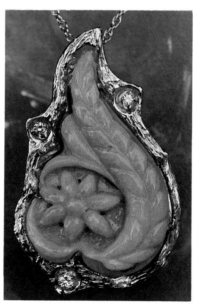

Photograph 16-3   Wayne Hadley

Brazilian opal carved by Wayne Hadley.

Popular jewelry-sized pieces include cameos, and freeform pendants. Large display pieces can have traditional oriental motifs or more modern western themes. The value of opal carvings has been quite perplexing to me. I expected that these carvings would have an opal value *plus* an addition for the workmanship and art of the carving. Unfortunately, after many years of dealing with all qualities and types of opal carvings, I have come to a different conclusion.

Opal carvings, even exceptional ones, often do not sell for as much as an oval cabochon of equal quality and size. They should, but they don't. I have no explanation for this, but it is a fact.

Photograph 16-4   *Morris Ratcliff*
Carved by Erwin Pauley in Idar Oberstein.
This frog is treated matrix opal.

In valuing a carved opal, value it as if it were a traditional opal cut in freeform shape. Pay particular attention to cracks as they are more common in carved pieces. Cracks are faulted heavily in jewelry carvings as they are in other cut opal. Cracks are not penalized as severely in large display pieces unless they interfere with the overall beauty of the piece. Enter a subtraction of -.30 for a crack which does not interfere with the beauty of a display carving. (See Section VII.) Use a large subtraction for more prominent cracks. An adjustment for the fact that the opal is carved rather than cabbed is made in the shape entry of Section VII of the Opal Evaluation Form. Note in Table 10-7 that values of +.10 to -.30 are given for carved opals. Adjust upward slightly (no more than +.10) if the carving is exceptional in workmanship and design. (See Photographs 16-3 and 16-4.) A downward adjustment should be made for poor workmanship and designs that are somewhat larger (to -.30). Anyone who has ever tried to sell a poorly carved opal will tell you how difficult it is even at a low price. Display carvings are often very large. Be sure to adjust the size weighting in Section VII as well.

Other Works of Art

Opal has been incorporated into many works of art. The possibilities are limited only by the artist's imagination. For example, the exceptional display knife, shown in Photograph 16-5, was produced by noted knife maker, Tim Herman. Made with opal cabochons set in 18kt gold handles, it sold recently for $15,000. A substantial portion of the price is accounted for by the two matching 2" x ½" solid opal cabs which form the handle.

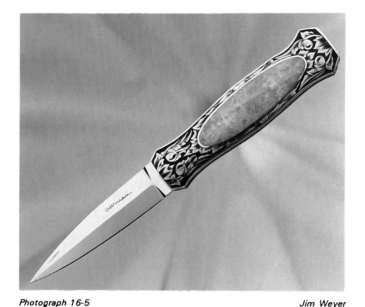

Photograph 16-5   *Jim Weyer*

Review

1. Intarsia is now being made into magnificent jewelry with quality opal center stones. Prices can range as high as $3,000.

2. Mosaic picture pendants are mass produced and inexpensive.

3. Carvings are true works of art, yet their artistic merit is not usually reflected adequately in their price. They are under-valued by today's market.

4. Other works of art employ opal as part of the design.

Chapter 17

Valuing Uncut Opal

The art and science of valuing rough (uncut) opal is even more complicated than valuing cut opal. Cutting involves a lot of guessing about what the final product will look like. And it involves a great deal of risk. To spite the best efforts of dealers in rough opal to sort them out, uncut opal always contains surprises. Some are good. Some are not. Cutters must be compensated for their skill *and* the risk. Cutting is fascinating, rewarding, and frustrating—sometimes all at once. I love it![42] In this chapter I hope to give you some appreciation of the relationship between cut and rough prices.

"I can buy this rough for $100 per gram and the man says the stones I cut will be worth $100 per carat. Is it a good buy?" The answer, I am afraid to say, is an unequivocal "It depends." It depends upon whether the cut stones really would be worth $100 per carat, but it also depends on much more. Suppose you bought 30 grams of the rough ($3,000). You would have to cut 30 carats of opal at $100 per carat to break even. And this does not compensate you for your cutting time or for the risk you take, or for marketing costs.

As always, the question of value is very complicated but I will try to make things as simple as possible. In the discussion that follows, I will take you step by step through the valuing process. I show you how to value rough given a cut stone value and how to estimate cut stone costs for any rough opal cost.

---

[42]For further information on cutting, obtain Paul B. Downing, *Opal Cutting Made Easy*, 1993.

Factors Which Affect
Rough Opal Value

Let's look at the factors which are important. Clearly, all the factors which make up the value of a cut stone—those listed and discussed in previous chapters: base color, fire color, fire intensity, fire pattern, cut, size of stones—are equally important in rough. But there are some additional factors as well.

> ## Most important is YIELD.

Yield is the number of carats of finished opal obtained from a parcel of rough. Yields are usually expressed as a percentage of the weight of the rough. A high-yield would be 40% or more, a low-yield would be below 20%. Since there are 5 carats in a gram, a low-yield of 20% means that the rough would produce 0.2 grams or one carat of cut opal per gram of rough. A high-yielding rough (40%) would produce two carats of cut opal (1 x .4 x 5 = 2).

TYPICAL PERCENT YIELD OF OPAL ROUGH

Yield	Type of Stone Cut	
	Freeform	Calibrated Ovals
Low	20	10
Medium	30	20
High	40	30

Yield will be higher when freeform stones are cut and lower for calibrated stones cut from the same rough. (See *Opal Cutting Made Easy*.) So when we talk about a high-yielding rough it means that you can get more finished weight (freeform or calibrated) per unit of rough weight. Yield for free size ovals, stones which are not standard sizes like 10 x 8mm but something like 13 x 9mm, fall somewhere near the middle in terms of yield. Each rough stone will provide a different yield. When assessing a number of stones (as in a parcel of rough), estimate the average yield for the whole batch. The preceding table shows approximate yields for various types of stones and cuts.

An equally important factor is RISK.

Risk is the probability that the rough will cut the finished opals it looks like it will cut. Cutting opal has its challenges. You must adjust to cracks and inclusions. You may find that the color is not as bright, or is more directional than you expected. But what makes it fun is that you may find a real beauty in the rough, something the miner didn't expect to turn out or which was hidden inside. Every risk should have its potential reward. As any economist will tell you, a risky investment should sell for less than one of certain yield. Likewise, risky rough should be cheaper than more certain material. Risky rough is material with frequent signs of cracks, or with potential sand inclusions, or with potential orientation problems (stones which are bright on the edge but may not be bright on the top). Risky rough is often the most fun because of the potential of a *super stone* hidden behind the sand. Risky rough produces big winners and sometimes big losers, but lots of fun. (I must admit I love to cut risky rough.)

CUTTING COST must be added.

Cutting Cost is the cost to you of having the rough cut to your specifications. I know, you cut the opal yourself so it costs you nothing. Not true. Your time is valuable. Yes, even if you are retired. You could be working at McDonald's or playing golf. Only you can decide what your time is worth.

Suppose your cutter can complete 7.5 carats in an hour. Then at $25 per hour your cutting cost is $3.33 per carat. Cutting cost increases if you are cutting small calibrated stones as they take more time per carat. Also, cutting cost increases with the value of the rough. I spend a lot of time looking and thinking when rough is particularly good. I may be slow but generally I find it difficult to cut more than 5 calibrated 10 x 8mm ovals per hour. At approximately 1.5 carats each, that's 7.5 carats per hour. At a 30% yield I would use 5 grams of opal. Thus the cutting cost would be $5 per gram (or $3.33 per carat of finished stones). Freeforms and larger ovals would be less costly to cut per gram and smaller calibrated stones would be more. Remember, it costs you the same to cut a $50 per gram rough as a $10 per gram rough of equal yield.

Finally, you must determine how much it will cost you to sell the cut stone. I have no real guidelines here as each situation will be different.

Example of
Valuing Rough Opal

One way to see how all of this fits together is to work backwards from the value of the cut stone. Let's say that you estimate that a parcel of opal will yield on average $10 per carat opals. How much is the rough worth per gram? Let's use high and low cases. Follow along with the example below:

ESTIMATED VALUE OF CUT STONES
= $10 PER CARAT

	Yield	
	High (40%)	**Low (20%)**
Carats Per Gram of Rough	2.00 carat/gram	1.00 carat/gram
Value of Rough	$20/per gram	$10/per gram

A low yield means that the cutter gets 1 carat per gram of rough. So, the most the rough would be worth is $10 per gram, since it will yield $10 worth of cut opal (1 carat). A high-yield makes the rough more valuable ($20 per gram [10 times 2.00] in the above example) because there are more carats to sell (or use).

Cutting Cost: Higher cutting cost ($6 per gram) follows from cutting calibrated sizes or rough that is difficult to cut. Cutting costs reduce the amount you would be willing to pay for the rough. The $5 figure discussed above is about average for me. Cutting cost can go to $4 per gram or lower in some cases where freeforms are cut.

Cutting Cost	$4 per gram (low)	$6 per gram (high)
Price of Rough	$16 per gram	$4 per gram

Risk - Next we must adjust for risk. Even if the stones are not very risky, you should assign a modest (20%) risk premium. A high risk (40%) may be needed in some cases. The risk adjusted rough price equals the value of the rough times one minus percent of the risk (4.00 x [1-.4] = 2.40).

Risk Factor	20%	40%
Risk Adjusted Rough Price	$12.80/gram	$2.40/gram

So, you can see that cut opals with an average value of $10 per carat can come from rough that ranges from $2.40 to $12.80 per gram. In fact, it can come from material much cheaper or much more expensive. Remember that beautiful opal you cut from a $2 piece out of a tray? Still this system can be used to estimate the rough price you might be willing to pay for a given quality stone.

If you wish to estimate the value of a piece of rough, the example above can be used as a guide. First, assess the characteristics most likely to be found in the cut stones from this rough. Will they be white base? Red multicolor? How bright? How big will the average stone be? After assessing all the characteristics that this rough opal is likely to exhibit, you can find the relevant Table from Chapter 10 and determine an estimated price per carat. Using the Opal Evaluation Form will help you here. Adjust for all the characteristics such as fire color, pattern, consistency, etc. Some will be hard to determine in the rough. That's why we put in the *risk factor*.

An Example of Estimating
Cost Per Carat

Now suppose you are faced with a rough at a specific price per gram and wish to assess the cost of cutting stones from it. All you need to do is to work the system backwards. Let's suppose that the rough is priced at $10 per gram; see below:

COST OF OPALS
CUT FROM ROUGH
PRICED AT $10 PER GRAM

	Low Quality	High Quality
Cost of Rough = $10 per gram		
Yield	20%	40%
Cost of Cut Opal Per Carat	$10 (1 ct)	$5.00 (2 ct)
Cutting Cost	$6 per gm	$4 per gm
Cost After Cutting	$ 16 /ct	$7.00 /ct*
Risk Premium	40%	20%
Risk Adjusted Cost of Cut Opal (Divide by 1 Minus Risk)	$20.00/ct	$8.75/ct

*Since Yield is two carats per gram.

Again you can see that the cost of the cut opal can vary considerably from different roughs of the same price per gram. The value of the finished stones would then be assessed as discussed above. Comparing the estimated value with the cost per carat of the stones cut from this rough will give you an answer to the question asked at the beginning of the chapter.

Some Practical Guidance

This is all very complex, isn't it? Fortunately, there is a simple rule of thumb which will allow you to produce an approximation. If a rough costs $10 per gram, the cut opals will cost about $10 per carat. Likewise, if you estimate that a rough will produce $10 per carat opals, it should cost $10 per gram on average. This one to one ratio can be used for any value. It includes modest cutting costs and risk costs. The rule should be adjusted for high- or low-yield rough. High-yield rough (rough that is expected to cut well) may be worth twice as much ($20 per gram) as the rule states. Low-yield rough may be worth only half as much ($5 per gram).

The discussion above is for an average of a number of stones. Suppose you bought an ounce of opal at $10 per gram and there were 8 stones in it. Some stones will cut well and be worth more than $10 per carat, but others may be worth less. You should not expect each stone to meet the rule.

In some cases dealers will sell individual uncut stones. When this is done, a premium over the price of an unselected lot is charged. The reason is obvious. The customer will pick out the best stones. Is it better to pick or to buy a lot? The answer depends upon the variation in quality among the rough stones and on the premium charged, as well as your purpose in cutting. A large variation in quality or a small premium suggests that picking might be a good idea. If you have a special purpose in mind, picking may be necessary.

There are types of rough which are generally better or worse than the average. Potch and color is usually risky, so it sells for less than you would expect. It is also more expensive to cut because of a lot of waste and relatively low-valued finished opals (on average). But it is great fun to cut! Other rough with strong lines of color and a lot of potch are also lower priced. Broad flash rough is more likely to not face as well. Orientation of color may also be a problem. This rough usually sells a little cheaper. Flat thin stones also sell cheaper because there is more likelihood of cracks and sand problems and because finished stones may be too thin to use as solids unless cut into small stones. However thin stones can make dynamite doublets, triplets, or small solids. The price of thin rough should be adjusted to reflect the value of the doublets or triplets you would expect to cut from it. And you need to deduct a little extra on the value of the rough to reflect the extra cutting cost and risk. On the other hand, thick stones with full color will sell at a premium because risk is low and yield is high.

Finally

Remember, this discussion is intended as a general guide. Use good judgment in each individual case.

Review

1. The value of rough is equal to the value of the finished stones it is expected to yield, adjusted for estimates of yield, risk, and cutting costs.
2. The estimation procedure can go either direction; from rough to finished or from finished to rough.
3. A simple rule of thumb is that the cost of the rough opal per gram equals the cost of the finished stone per carat.

Chapter 18

Conclusions

Well, that about does it. You now have a good sense of what each characteristic is about and what all these terms really mean. You know how to identify and characterize a stone correctly and, if I have done my job well, your characterization will be the same as mine. You have the light you need to do a consistent job. And you know how to put it all together to estimate the value of an opal.

You have learned a lot and I am proud of you.

Still, you may be saying to yourself, "I don't have great confidence that I am doing things right." The only way to build that confidence is to look at a lot of opals. You will, because you know so much more about them now. You'll study opals at shows and understand so much more because you will know what you are looking for. Rings and pendants that people wear will stand out. Periodically you will notice something you haven't seen before and ask about it, sorting through the inevitable conflicting opinions to reach the truth. Step-by-step your knowledge will grow. You are on your way to becoming an opal expert!

Another way to get exposure to a lot of opals is to take the *Opal Evaluation Classes* I offer from time to time. They give you hands-on experience. You will refine your knowledge; learning from me and your fellow classmates. And I will learn too.

This is not *the end*. We both have so much more to learn about opal. One lifetime is nowhere near enough. When I talk to people who have lived opal all their life, like Australian experts Len Cram and Greg Sherman, I realize how much more there is to know. For even they are still learning. It is a fascinating and challenging subject. Learning gives you a good excuse to appreciate the most beautiful gemstone in the world, *The Opal*.

In reading and using this book you will come upon discussions that you may not understand or which you feel could have been presented more clearly. I would love to hear from you so that I might make subsequent editions even better.

Good luck—and have fun!

Photograph 18-1

Rudy Weber

Bibliography

American Opal Society, "Opal Appraisal Kit," American Opal Society, 1985, Xeroxed.

Anonymous, "Black Opal From Brazil," *Gems & Gemology*, Spring, 1991, p. 49.

Anonymous, "Black Cat's-Eye Opal From Jalisco, Mexico," *Gems & Gemology*, Winter, 1990, p. 304.

Anonymous, "Cat's-eye Opal," *Gems & Gemology*, Fall, 1990, p. 232.

Anonymous, "Opals with an Unusual Inclusion," *Gems & Gemology*, Fall, 1990, p. 222.

Anonymous, "Plastic-coated sugar-treated opal," *Gems & Gemology*, Fall, 1990, p. 236.

Anonymous, "Michelsen Gemstone Index, Wholesale Diamond & Colored Stone Pricing Guide," *Gem Spectrum*, 1991.

Anonymous, *Opal Certificate*, The Australian Gem Industry Assoc., No Date.

Anonymous, *The Gemstone Enhancement Manual*, Jewelers of America, July, 1990.

Australian Gem Industry Association, "Opal Prices: Still Going Up," *Jewelers' Circular - Keystone*, August, 1991, pp. 148-152.

Barbour, Tom R. & Barbour, Joyce, "Country of Opals-Honduras," *Lapidary Journal*, November, 1964, pp. 948-955.

Brown, Grahame, "Treated Andamooka Matrix Opal," *Gems & Gemology*, Summer, 1991, pp. 100-106.

Burch, C. R., "A Re-Examination of Slocum Stone with Particular Emphasis on Inclusions," *Journal of Gemology*, 1985, pp. 586-596.

Campbell, Deborah Ann, "Fiery Opals in Southern California," *Gems and Minerals*, March, 1983, pp. 37-62.

Cody, Andrew, "Valuation of Australian Precious Opal," *Gemological Association of Australia*, 1988.

Cody, Andrew, *Australian Precious Opals*, Andrew Cody Pty. Ltd., 1991.

Colen, Mark, "The Fire of Opal," *Rock & Gem*, Oct, 1991, pp. 24-31.

Cram, Len, *Beautiful Australian Opals*, Robert Brown & Assoc. Pty Ltd., Australia, 1990.

Cram, Len, *Beautiful Lightning Ridge*, Robert Brown & Assoc. Pty Ltd., Australia, 1991.

Cram, Len, *Beautiful Queensland Opals*. Robert Brown & Assoc. Pty Ltd., Australia, 1991.

Cuthbert, Donna L., "Precious Opal In Idaho," *Lapidary Journal*, October, 1969, pp. 928-930.

Dietz, Ralph W., "Play of Colors in Precious Opal," *Gems and Minerals*, June, 1965, pp. 16-18.

Downing, Paul B., "An Australian Love Affair," *Lapidary Journal*, June, 1989, pp. 32-40.

Downing, Paul B., *Opal Cutting Made Easy*, Majestic Gems & Carvings, Inc., 1984.

Downing, Paul B., "Australian Opal Discoveries," *Rock & Gem*, September, 1990, pp. 48-51.

Downing, Paul B., *Opal Adventures*, Majestic Gems & Carvings, Inc., 1990.

Downing, Paul B., "Evaluating Cut Opal," *Rock & Gem*, December, 1987, pp. 16-21.

Downing, Paul B., "World Opal Supply and Prices," *Rock & Gem*, September, 1986.

Downing, Paul B., "Homegrown Precious Opal," *Rock & Gem*, December, 1988, pp. 36-39.

Downing, Paul B., "Valuing Cut Opal," *Cornerstone*, July, 1990.

Drucker, Richard, *The Guide*, Gemworld International, 1991.

Duncan, Mike, "Crazing of Stones," *Gemline, Australian Gem Industry Association*, October, 1988.

Dunn, Pete J., "Observations on the Slocum Stone," *Gems & Gemology*, Winter, 1976-1977, pp. 252-256.

Federman, David, "Fire Opal: Pride of Mexico," *Modern Jeweler*.

Fritsch, Emmanuel and Rossman, George, "An Update on Color in Gems. Part 3: Colors Caused by Bend Gaps and Physical Phenomena," *Gems & Gemology*, Summer, 1988, pp. 81-102.

Gauthier, Jean-Pierre, "L'opal Noble an Microscope Electronique," Xerox, 1991.

GIA, *Gem Reference Guide*, Gemological Institute of America, 1988.

GIA, "Phenomenal Gems, Colored Stones Lesson 37," *Gemological Institute of America*, 1989.

GIA, "Colored Stone Course, Assignment 17," Gemological Institute of America, 1990.

Griffith, Jossie, "Arizona Blue Opal Goes to Europe," *Lapidary Journal*, November, 1980, pp. 1750-1754.

Gubelin, Eduard, "Lightning Ridge—Die Wiege der australischen Schwarzopale," *Lapis*, February, 1988, pp. 15-30.

Hadley, Wayne, "Carving Opal," *Rock & Gem*, September, 1990, pp. 52-55.

Hadley, Wayne, "A Carved Opal Pendant," *Rock & Gem*, September, 1985, pp. 33-35.

Hadley, Wayne, "Carving Opal," *Rock & Gem*, September, 1986, pp. 28-35.

Hadley, Wayne, "Gemstone Carvings," *Rock & Gem*, January, 1988, pp. 53-55.

Heylman, Edgar B., "The Magdalena Opal District," *Gems and Minerals*, June, 1984, pp. 54-57.

Heylman, Edgar B., "Varieties of Mexican Opal," *Lapidary Journal*, August, 1984, pp. 746-742.

Heylman, Edgar B., "Virgin Valley," *Lapidary Journal*, June, 1987, pp. 33-44.

Hiss, Deborah Ann, "Opal: The Down Under Wonder," *Lizzadro Museum*, Summer-Fall, 1990.

Holmes, Irwan, "Fireworks at Midnight on the Isle of Java," *Opal Express*, July, 1986, pp. 3-6.

Huett, Dale E., "A Centenial Celebration - Gem Quality Opal in Oregon," *Lapidary Journal*, November, 1990, pp. 22-30.

Jones, Bob, "Idaho Blue Fire Opal," *Rock & Gem*, February, 1989, pp. 56-59.

Kammerling, R. & Weldon, R., "Microscopic Features of Imitation Phenomenal Gems, Part 2: Plastic Imitations," *Colored Stone*, March/April, 1990.

Kammerling, R, Koivula, J., and Kane, R., "Gemstone Enhance ment and Its Detection in the 1980s," *Gems & Gemology*, Spring, 1990, p. 35.

Koivula, J. & Kammerling, R., "Opalite: Plastic Imitation Opal with True Play-of-Color," *Gems & Gemology*, Spring, 1989, pp.30-34.

Koivula, John I., Kammerling, Robert C. & Weldon, Robert, "Microscopic Features of Imitation Phenomenal Gems," *Colored Stone*, March/April, 1990.

Kurtzeman, Jeff, "Conk Opal," *Rock & Gem*, pp. 76-77.

Leechman, Frank, *The Opal Book*, Ure Smith Pty. Ltd., 1961

Lyons, Diana D. H., "Black Opal Prices Stabilized," *Colored Stone*, September/October, 1989, pp. 8-14.

Manson, D. Vincent, "Plastic Impregnated Gem Opal," *Gems & Gemology*, Summer, 1978, pp. 49-57.

Nassau, K., "Gemstone Imitations Made of Glass, Ceramics, Plastic and Composites," *Lapidary Journal*, March, 1980, pp. 2528-2530.

Nassau, Kurt, "Opal Treatments," *Lapidary Journal*, June, 1989, pp. 44-51.

O'Leary, Barrie, *A Field Guide To Australian Opals*, Gemcraft Publications, Pty. Ltd., 1977.

Opal Spectrum, "Opal As An Investment," *Lapidary Journal*, October, 1977, pp. 1492-1493.

Pough, Frederick H., "Spectral Gemstones, Frozen Rainbows," *Lapidary Journal*, September, 1985, pp. 19-21.

Shaub, B. M., "The Origin of Fire Opals," *Rock & Gem*, August, 1987, pp. 36-39.

Shendenhelm, W. R. C., "The Value of Opal," *Rock & Gem*, September, 1984, pp. 20-21.

Sinkankas, John, *Sinkankas' Catalog of Gem Values*, Geoscience Press, 1968.

Skalicky, Jiri, "Interesting Opals From Czechosolovakia," *Lapidary Journal*, July, 1983, pp. 578-584.

Smith, Kevin Lane, "Opals from Opal Butte, Oregon," *Gems & Gemology*, Winter, 1988, pp. 229-236.

Smith, Christopher P., "Unusual Natural Opal," *Gems & Gemology*, Spring, 1990, pp. 96-97.

Spendlove, Earl, "Gilson Synthetic Opal," *Rock & Gem*, September, 1988, pp. 37-39.

Spendlove, Earl, "Star Opal," *Rock & Gem*, September, 1986, pp. 36-39.

Spendlove, Earl, "Idaho Opal," *Rock & Gem*, October, 1991, pp.32-39.

Thompson, Michael, "Appraisal-Writing Software: More Than Just Pretty Reports," *Jewelers' Circular-Keystone*, February, 1991, pp. 226-236.

Walker, W. H., "Black Opal Matrix," *Gems and Minerals*, September, 1963, pp. 35-37.

Wise, Richard W., "Australia, Thy Name is Opal," *Colored Stone*, March/April, 1991, pp. 6-9.

Wood, John, "The World's Largest Opal," *Rock & Gem*, December, 1990, pp. 53-54.

Zeitner, June Culp, "Querataro Opals," *Lapidary Journal*, June, 1987, pp. 20-26.

Zeitner, June Culp & Bernhardt, Ute, "An Important New Opal Carving," *Lapidary Journal*, February, 1980, pp. 2324-2346.

Zeitner, June, "The Opal of Querataro," *Lapidary Journal*, July, 1979, pp. 868-880.

Glossary of Terms

Andamooka - A mining area in South Australia which produces crystal opal and treating matrix opal.

Assembled Opal - Opal that has been glued together, either with other opal or another material. (See Doublets and Triplets.)

Baroque - An opal cut in an irregular outline with curved sides; a variety of freeform.

Base Color - The background color of the opal.

Black Crystal - A solid opal which is translucent to transparent with play of color which when viewed from the top is graded as at least number 3 black on the Lightning Ridge Miners Association Tone Scale.

Black Opal - A solid opal which is opaque when viewed from the top of the stone and which has a play of color against a dark background, graded as at least number 3 black on the Lightning Ridge Miners Association Tone Scale.

Blue Opal - A solid opal which has a blue base color.

Boulder Brown - A natural boulder opal with crystal or semi-crystal opal on a brown ironstone background.

Boulder White - A natural boulder opal with opaque white or other base color opal on an ironstone background.

Boulder Doublets - A two-part assembled stone made of precious opal with an ironstone backing glued to it.

Boulder Black - A natural boulder opal which faces as a black opal as defined with the Lightning Ridge Miners Association Tone Scale.

Boulder Opal - A seam or patches of solid opal still attached to the parent rock in which the opal is found.

Boulder Matrix - A combination of opal and ironstone where the opal is mixed through the ironstone rather than in seams.

Brightness of Fire - The intensity of light in the fire coming back as the light is diffracted from the opal.

Broad Flashfire - A fire pattern in which sheets of fire color cover a large section or all of the opal's surface.

Brown Crystal - A solid opal which has a transparent brown base color.

Calibrated - Opals cut to standard dimensions.

Clarity - The degree of transparency of an opal.

Clarity Cross - A black cross on a white background used to measure the degree of clarity of an opal.

Common Opal - Opal which does not show a play of color in a distinct pattern. Stones showing general opalescence only are common opal.

Concrete - Clay naturally cemented together with common or precious opal; found in Andamooka and usually dyed.

Conk Opal - A matrix opal from Nevada where opal has filled openings left by fungus which attack a Douglas fir before it was buried and silicified.

Consistency - Sameness in all the relevant characteristics of an opal, including color, pattern, density of fire, and density and color of the background.

Contra Luz Opal - An opal which shows a play of color when viewed from the front with the light passing through the stone from the back.

Coober Pedy - A mining area in South Australia most known for its white base opals.

Cracked Opal - Opal with one or more breaks in the solid opal resulting from pressure.

Crazed Opal - Opal which shows a multitude of little cracks interwoven into a spider web-like design.

Crystal Opal - A solid opal which is transparent as graded by the *Clarity Cross*.

Cut - The overall shape and quality of cutting.

Directionality of Fire - The degree to which an opal's fire is of the same brightness when viewed from various angles.

Dome - The arch of the top of an opal; divided into high, medium, and low (flat).

Dominant Color - The most important fire color in a particular opal.

Doublet - A two-part stone consisting of a precious opal glued to another stone; either opal or some other material.

Dyed Opal - Opal treated with chemicals to dye it black in order to give it an appearance similar to black opal.

Dyed Matrix - A porous matrix opal from Andamooka that is dyed black using a sugar and sulfuric acid process.

Fire Color - The color or combination of colors which are produced when light is diffracted out of the opal.

Fire Pattern - The pattern made by the play of color in the opal.

Fire Opal - A solid opal with a transparent orange to red-orange base color. More properly referred to as "orange crystal opal."

Flashfire - A fire pattern showing irregular chunks of fire, no one of which covers a large percentage of the opal.

Free Size - Opals cut as ovals but not cut to standard dimensions.

Freeform - An opal cut into any irregular outline.

Gilson Opal - A synthetic opal originated by Pierre Gilson.

Gray Opal - A solid opal which is opaque with a gray base color corresponding to the gray tones on the Lightning Ridge Miners Association Tone Scale.

Harlequin - A fire pattern which shows square or angular blocks of fire set closely together.

Hydrophane - Opal with a porous structure which absorbs water. White when dry, often transparent when wet. Sometimes dyed.

Imitation Opal - See *Simulant*.

Inclusions - Non-opal or common opal within the natural opal.

Intarsia - A work of art in which gemstones are carefully fit together to produce an intricate geometric design.

Jelly Opal - A solid opal which is transparent showing no play of color. It may show an opalescence without a fire pattern.

Lightning Ridge - A mining area in New South Wales which is famous for its black opals.

Lines of Color - Precious opal formed in one or more relatively flat layers, usually with common opal between the precious opal.

Man-made Opal - See *Synthetic Opal*.

Matrix Opal - Opal mixed throughout a parent rock.

Milk Opal - See *White Opal*.

Mintabie - A mining area in South Australia noted for its black seam opal, but which now produces mostly crystal opal.

Mosaic Opal - A form of doublet or triplet where small pieces of opal are fit together to cover the face of the stone.

Mosaic Opal Pictures - A mosaic opal triplet which has a painted glass placed over it to produce a picture.

Multicolor - An opal having at least three distinct fire colors.

Night Stone - An opal which shows a very bright play of color in low light.

Nobby - A roundish opal found in the clay of Lightning Ridge.

Noble Opal - Precious opal.

Opal Brightness Kit - A set of opals of various brightness used as a standard against which to measure the brightness of any particular opal.

Opalite - A plastic opal simulant.

Orange Opal - A solid opal which is translucent to opaque with an orange to red-orange base color.

Orange Crystal Opal - A solid opal which is transparent with an orange to red-orange base color.

Painted Lady - A boulder opal consisting of precious opal on tan quartzite found in Andamooka; often painted to depict a scene.

Picture Stone - Opals which create a picture with fire, sometimes in conjunction with inclusions, that reminds one of a specific object.

Pineapple - Opal replacing a crystal mass that looks like the leaves on the top of a pineapple.

Pinfire - A fire pattern consisting of small pinpoint circles of fire.

Potch Opal - Another term for common opal.

Precious Opal - Opal which displays a play of color in a distinct pattern.

Rare Patterns - Rare or unusual fire patterns which do not fit easily into the pinfire, flashfire, broad flashfire, or harlequin fire pattern definitions.

Rolling Flashfire - A fire pattern in which sheets of fire roll across the surface of the opal as it is moved.

Rough Opal - Opal in its natural state before it has been shaped and polished.

Semi-Black - A solid opal which is translucent to opaque with a play of color against a dark gray background corresponding to the semi-black tone on the Lightning Ridge Miners Association Tone Scale.

Semi-Crystal - A solid opal which is translucent as graded by the *Clarity Cross*.

Shell Doublets - A boulder doublet in which the precious opal is from opalized clam shells found in Coober Pedy.

Simulant - Non-opal materials produced by man to simulate natural opals.

Slocum Stone - An opal simulant made in Detroit, Michigan by John Slocum.

Solid Opal - Consisting only of opal with no other type of stone present and naturally occurring in one piece (not glued together).

Split Face Boulder - Boulder opal which has been split at the seam to expose opal on both faces of the split seam.

Structure Lines - Lines in an opal where the internal structure of the opal, the size and/or alignment of the silica spheres, has changed. Not a crack.

Sun Stone - An opal which shows a play of color only in bright sunlight.

Synthetic - Opal grown in a laboratory.

Treated Opal - Any opal which has been altered by the introduction of chemicals after it was mined. (See *Dyed Opal*.)

Triplet - A three-part stone with a precious opal center, a clear cap, and a darkened base.

Type of Opal - Common types of opal are solid opal, boulder opal, matrix opal, assembled opals (doublets and triplets), treated (dyed) opal, synthetic opal, and opal simulants.

Value - Market value set by a willing buyer and a willing seller.

Weight - The weight of a cut opal, usually measured in carats.

White Cliffs - A mining area in New South Wales which produced the first find of crystal opal in the 1890s.

White Opal - A solid opal which is opaque with a white or off-white base color.

Yowah - A mining area in Queensland which produces an unusual boulder matrix opal known as a Yowah Nut.

Photographic Credits

I wish to thank the following photographers for allowing me to use their work.

Len Cram - Lightning Ridge, N.S.W., Australia

Tony Dabdoub - New Orleans, LA

Keith Griffin - Scott, LA

Wayne Hadley - Marysville, WA

Tino Hammid - Los Angeles, CA. Photographs courtesy of Jim's Gems, Wayne, NJ

Keith Hodson - Scottsdale, AZ

Manning International - New York, NY

Gerald Pauley - Melbourne, Australia

Morris Ratcliffe - Courtesy of Hazel Ratcliffe LeSuer (deceased)

John Slocum - Detroit, MI

Walch & Williams - Elkadar, IA

Rudy G. Weber - Australian Opal & Gemstone Photographic Library, Sydney, Australia. Items photographed courtesy of:

Andrew Cody	Majestic Gems & Carvings
Aussie Opal & Gem	Percy Marks
Bentine Gems	Nat Luft
Joy Clayton	Opal Australia
Gemstone Boutique	Opal Beauty
Jackson Opal	Richard Osmond
K. Lehmann	Sherman Opal
Karen Lindley	George Simos
Madson Opal	

Jim Weyer - Courtesy of Tim Herman, Overland Park, KS

Index

Other Books by the Same Author

Look what reviewers are saying about *Opal Adventures*:

"This is the most complete book about opal that has been published in many years...The author takes the reader on exciting visits to such places as Coober Pedy, Mintabie and Lightning Ridge...Anyone...will enjoy this book and, after putting it down, will be tempted to call his travel agent."
June Culp Zeitner, *Lapidary Journal*

"*Opal Adventures*" would be the most complete up-to-date book on opal I have read for many, many years...All very enjoyable reading, with much to be learned by the reader." Grahame Brown, *Australian Gemologist*

Jeweler's Book Club, *JCK* rates *Opal Adventures* one of the 12 most highly acclaimed new books in its 1992 catalog and calls it "entertaining and educational."

Other Books by the Same Author

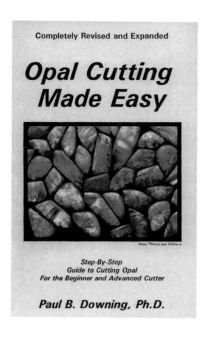

Completely Revised and Expanded

Opal Cutting Made Easy

Step-By-Step
Guide to Cutting Opal
For the Beginner and Advanced Cutter

Paul B. Downing, Ph.D.

Opal Cutting Made Easy
$5.95 - Revised 1993
100 pg 14 Color - 33 B&W
ISBN: 0-9625311-4-6

A proven step-by-step approach to cutting opal. Takes the beginner through the first stone; going on to explain advanced cutting techniques, including doublet and triplet making. Tips on how to buy rough opal. Easy to follow instructions.

ALSO AVAILABLE:
A companion 35 minute *Video* (VHS only) $29.95 shows you how to cut opal. It contains visual aids for procedures not easily explained in words. Professionally produced.

What some reviewers are saying about *Opal Cutting Made Easy*:

"If you would like to learn how to cut opal, do use this book...Effective...Well written...A very usable guide...A very worthwhile book."

Grahame Brown, *Australian Gemologist*

"Opal cutting taught in well-made tape...A professional job...highly recommended."

F. H . Pough, Ph.D. *Jewelers Book Club News*

ORDER FORM

No.	Title of Publication	Price	Total
	Opal Adventures	$19.95	$
	Opal Cutting Made Easy	$5.95	$
	Opal Cutting Made Easy Video	$29.95	$
	1 Title - Shipping (U.S. Mail)		$ 3.00
	2 or more titles - Shipping		$ 5.00
	INTERNATIONAL SHIPPING		$ 10.00
	TOTAL DUE		$

Mail to: **Majestic Press**, Inc. P. O. Box 2265, Estes Park, CO 80517-2265
(800) 468-0324